To: THE O[...]
MOTORSPORTS [...]

GW00993166

THANK YOU.
RICK SHORTLE
THE 1986 WINNER OF.
BRANDS HATCH
POST TWO MARSHALLS TROPHY

R Short
Rick
06/08/2022

FULL CIRCLE

An Autobiography

Patrick Shortle

authorHOUSE®

AuthorHouse™ UK
1663 Liberty Drive
Bloomington, IN 47403 USA
www.authorhouse.co.uk
Phone: 0800.197.4150

Published by AuthorHouse 02/27/2017

ISBN: 978-1-4520-5586-2 (sc)
ISBN: 978-1-4918-8508-6 (e)

Print information available on the last page.

This book is printed on acid-free paper.

Chapter 1.
Orchard Way. (The Huts)

My earliest recollection was in 1949, when I was 4yrs of age, we were living in Cranbrook. Kent, a small Country Town and known as the Garden of England, Cranbrook like most little towns and villages have changed out of all recognition, now they are full of little coffee houses, boutiques and designer shops.

Because we still have Brothers, Sisters, relatives, and friends in and around that area, we quite often go to Cranbrook.

Visiting Cranbrook will always give us a buzz! We love to sit outside a coffee house, trying to recognise people as they pass by, quite often we do, with the help of Hazel, who is my wife's Sister, and why is it when Hazel points out someone, and says, remember him you were at school together, your immediate reaction is, God he looks Old and can't accept you look the same too.

Cranbrook has become one of the "in places" it must cost a fortune to live there now, the Town is so lively, the high street is a nightmare, with all the double parking, gone the days, when you could walk the length of the high street without seeing a car.

As you read this book you will notice I do tend to go off on a tangent, and then come back to the subject I was talking about in the first place, anyway where was I? 4yrs of age, at the time we were one of several families, that were given our own accommodation, just a mile out of Cranbrook, it was called Orchard Way, before then, we lived with my Mum's parents at Branden, just over the road from Sissinghurst Castle, which is a couple of miles, the other side of Cranbrook.

Our accommodation was certainly nothing grand, basically all they were, was ex army Huts, made of corrugated sheeting, heating was a wood burning stove, that's all, but as kids I can't remember ever complaining about being cold, we moved a couple of times, whilst we were there, our first hut was number 10, and the best thing about that one, was our bedroom backed onto the farmers apple orchard, which produced Beauty of Bath apples, I can still imagine, the smell and taste to this day.

It's strange, although we were all living in what could only be described as very poor conditions, there was still a pecking order, the posh end and us, I'm sure the posh end wouldn't mind me mentioning their names.

One family were the Fosters and one of the Lads, Mick Foster ended up being a school buddies of mine, when he left school he joined the Navy, we would hate him coming home on leave, because the girls would gather around him like Bees around a Honey Pot, he then became a fireman, and I think a long distance lorry driver, before emigrating to Australia some 30yrs ago, and in 2005 he tracked me down through friends re-united, we now keep in touch on a weekly basis, we will one of these days, go and visit him and his wife Janice.

Another family was the Masters, for whatever reason we thought they were German spies, it of course turned out they were just ordinary people, but at the time, it was very exciting for all of us kids.

And then there was the Evers, a very prim and proper family, they lived the other end of the camp, their Son Tony, became a Plasterer just like my good self, and for a short while actually worked for me.

When we first moved to Orchard Way there was Mum, Dad, My Brother David and Me (Rick). We did have another Brother, Malcolm but he sadly died at six months of Bronchitis, he was born between David and myself, I don't really remember anything about Malcolm, as I was only two yrs old at the time The war had only been over for 4yrs, so there was still a lot of military evidence around, and National Service was still in force. Dad (William) but known as Bill, had just come out of the Air Force, and as far as I know he was a rear Gunner, quite a dangerous job I believe, Mum (Evelyn) but know as Babs, had also finished her stint in the WRAF, that's where she met Bill. Apparently Mum was a bit of a looker. We have a great photo of mum in her WRAF's uniform hanging proudly on our lounge wall.

Mum in her WRAF uniform

David and I were so excited, about living there, we thought it was a fantastic place, it was quite a small camp I think in all about 16 huts, nicely nestled between Apple trees, hence the name.

The Huts or Tin Town with Rick and Brother David

We soon made friends with the other kids, and before to long we were planning and dreaming up all sorts of crazy things. We nicknamed Orchard Way, the Huts or Tin Town for obvious reason. At the other end (the Masters end) us kids decided to build a camp on an area we called the hillside, the bigger boys decided to dig a big hole in the ground, then lay all all sorts of rubbish over the hole, to form a roof, we then put all the earth that was dug out of the hole on top, and used it as an hide away, you wouldn't have know there was this big hole underneath, we were lucky not to have been suffocated. To think about it now, I grimace, it must have looked bloody awful just like a shanty town, it's not surprising the Masters were not too pleased.

Another thing we did during the School summer hols was to get together, and build some soap boxes and have races, the private road leading to Orchard Way, was dead straight with an incline perfect for soap box races, again we used to beg pinch and borrow all sorts of things to get the show on the road, One chap slightly older than us called George Oliver, was our hero, his soap box or Bodge as we called them, to us was a Formula One, we had so much fun thro the summer hols, doing this, although some of us did get into trouble, and one lad pinched the wheels of his Mum pram, which she never found out about, until she had another baby, then all hell was let loose.

My Brother David is 2yrs younger than me, so although he was excited about living at Tin Town, he was at this moment in time, just a tad too young to be one of the Lads just yet, but his time will come.

We moved to Tin Town in the spring of 49, I was five in the July, school beckoned in the Sept, we never had much, I vaguely remember Mum talking to Dad about clothes she had to get me for school. The next few months were just like the last, not a care in the world, getting the odd thick ear from Mum and the neighbours, scrumping, going to Angley Woods. To us, it was all good harmless fun.

My Dad worked at Benenden Chest Hostpital, a place where they cared for the soldiers when they became ill, I never did know what sort of job it was, Mum said he was a Doctor, so left it at that, we used to stand at the top of the road and wait for Dad to come home, one particular day I will never forget, it was a hot sunny day, and I was there with David, waiting for Dad, I was throwing stones up in the air, quite big stones, Mum repeatedly told me to stop doing it, you could hurt someone, but I kept chucking the stones in the air, and seconds before Dad arrived home I through this stone in the air.

It came down and hit Mum on her forehead, she dropped to the ground I think I knocked her out, and still do not know to this day, if I did or not.

At that very second I knew I was in big trouble, but never realised just how angry my Dad was, at first naturally it was all about, was Mum ok, so I had a stay of execution, but not for long, when we got home I got the hiding of my life, as if that was not enough, he locked me up in the wardrobe, which seemed to last for hours, I was terrified, and rest assured I never threw anything around my Mum again.

Time past and all was forgotten, However I think Mum had other things to worry about, not that I knew there was anything wrong, but Dad and Mum split up just before I was due to start School, I think it was six of one and half a dozen of the other, although it was a bit more complicated than that, but for now we will leave it there.

With Dad gone things got very hard for Mum, but she was a survivor and somehow we seemed to get through.

September 1950 my first day at school, the only thing I could recall, was my footwear, I had black boots, we called clob hoppers, they were far too big for me, my short grey trousers were hand me downs as were my boots, from a friend of Mums, mind you I was clean as a whistle, and my clothes were clean if nothing else, one of the things I used to hate, was when Mum noticed a grubby mark on my face, she would pull a hankie out from inside her sleeve, spit on it then begin to rub the mark off, she would rub so hard my face was left sore and very red, I think this was a normal procedure from our Mums for all us lads. I don't remember to much about Primary school, probably because I didn't enjoy it, however I can recall on several occasions going to school, and then turning around and going back home, it wasn't too long before a man from the school came to our house, he would knock on the door, whilst I hid behind the settee, this happened a number of times, till my Mum found out, then there was all hell to pay.

Cranbrook Primary School

Also in 1950 the Queen did a visit, it seemed like the whole of Cranbrook made their way to the High Street and Stone Street, both sides were at least three deep, we were at school that day so our teacher Mrs Ralph escorted us in an orderly two by two line, waving little flags down to the Town, which was only a short walk, we made our way along Jockey Lane, which dropped down quite steeply from the school, past the Chip shop on the left, we would pop in there many many times on the way home from school to see if they had any bits and pieces we called them scraps, or crackling, they were lovely, amazing how bits of crispy batter and burnt chips were so enjoyable. As we got ever nearer we could hear the excitement from the crowd, Jockey Lane, arrives at the High Street, where the road does a 90 degree right hand turn, at that point it's known as Stone Street, we waved our flags even faster as we arrived at the High Street, our school was allocated a space outside White's the Bakers, we were lucky enough to have the best side of the High Street, the pavement on our side was well raised from the road, about four or so feet, unlike the other side of the road the pavement was level with the road, it was a fantastic atmosphere a real carnival setting, needless to say we were waiting, for which seemed like hours before the Queen's car passed by, all I can remember is that famous wave of hers, it was all over in seconds, but a great day for Cranbrook.

Although I never enjoyed the classroom side of Primary School, I excelled in sports, I was the best at 100yds sprint, and my speciality was the sack race, I had the advantage of being small, so I could put a foot in each corner of the sack ran like buggery, and was never beaten. I was also Goal-keeper for the school, and still have a school photo to this day of our football team, which is proudly next to my Grandson Cameron's Team football photo, and he's the goal-keeper too, I never found the subjects difficult, just boring, and to be honest this how it was going to be, for the rest of my school days.

Primary School Football Team, I'm sitting on the far left,

Primary School Sports Team I'm in middle row far left.

I also enjoyed having fun with my mates at playtime, this very often ran over into the classroom too, but a clip round the ear from the Teacher soon stopped that, I had a couple of girlfriends, Nora Seal was my favourite, and I remember on one occasion saying something like I will show you mine if you show me yours, mind you we were only six. As I said earlier I really don't have much to say about Primary school, but now and again the odd memory pops up, every year someone would visit to check us out for head lice etc. and I remember the Lady that used check us, would you believe it was, Mrs bugsby, hows that for a coincidence?

The Dentist would come to the school in those days, something I used to dread, this put me off seeing the Dentist for years, it took me 30yrs of adult life to pluck up the courage to go and see the dentist, I'm now fine and go every six months.

What terrified me was the awful smell of rubber, together with a mask they would put over your nose and mouth, until you drifted away so they could do what they had to do, I could smell the mask for days.

One thing that never seemed to happen was bullying everyone most of the time seemed to get on with each other.

So that was Primary School, It seemed as if I was there a lifetime, when in reality it was only six years, we all sat for the Eleven Plus which decided whether you went to Grammar School, Technical College, or the normal Secondary school which is where I landed up.

Although Primary School to me was a bit boring, my time after School and at weekends never seemed to be, we always found someway of getting into mischief. Now I was at the ripe old age of seven, Mum said I could go hop picking, something Mum did every year. It wasn't a case of going hop picking, I actually had my own half a bin, the only thing I can recall about hop picking before I was seven, was sitting on a five bar farm gate playing the mouth organ, when all of a sudden I looked down and in the hedge were loads of Grass Snakes Adders slithering about, I was absolutely terrified, I can remember to this day, running for all I was worth over the hop mounds that separated each hop row, I was screaming for my Mum, and to this very day I cannot stand to even look at them, even if they are on the TV I have to look away.

Brother David in the pram with big Brother Rick standing next to the War Memorial.

We would pick the hops at Enfield's Farm, which was just down the road, opposite the war memorial, So there I was seven years of age with my first job, a half a bin, which basically was a full hop bin with a section of Hessian sown in, so 2 pickers had half each, a hop bin was about eight foot long, and the best way to describe it, it looks like a very long bath made out of Hessian, the Hessian sack type bath was fixed to a wooden frame which had two handles a bit like a rickshaw at each end, for moving along the hop row. I loved hop picking, and although I never got the money, it had to go towards buying my school uniform, even at that age I was quite competitive and would do my damdest to try and pick more than my mate who had the other half of the bin, but to be fair he was easy to beat, he spent most of the time, running off and playing with his mates, we would queue up at the farm office on a weekly basis for our money; I enjoyed this as I felt grown up, even though I never saw hide or hair of the dosh. Hop picking was the last two weeks of August, and the first two or three weeks in September, which meant I missed a bit of school, you could get way with it in those days.

It was getting near November 5th Bonfire-night, and needles to say all us kids at Tin Town got together and built the biggest bonfire we could, it wasn't hard to find stuff to burn, the neighbours always had a pile of rubbish in their gardens, and I suppose it was a welcome date in the calendar for the parents, to have a good clearout, the downside to us Kids, the lighting of the fire, and the evening had to be supervised by adults, and it was always Mr Masters, to us Kids it was the worse choice possible, but to be honest looking at it now from an adults perspective, it was the best choice.

We always started to build the bonfire weeks before the event, it was exciting and a major operation, there was a guy to burn too, the evening was always a success whatever the weather, we would put apples and potatoes in the fire all, as black as your hat when we ate them, but to us they were the business. As usual we were unable to have much in the way of a firework display, but to be fair all the parents clubbed together, so at least we had something.

All us Kids were getting excited about Bonfire-night, we even had a programme of events, mainly to make the fireworks last as long as possible, I know it seems daft, but to us, the day after Bonfire-night was almost as exciting as the night itself, we would all be out by the Bonfire at the crack of dawn, pushing and poking the still warm embers, to see if we could get any life back into it, but the most important bit was to see if we could find any fireworks that never went off, those that we did find, would be opened up, pouring the powder onto a flat surface, then strike a match so it flared up, no health and safety in those days.

However little did we know, but this Bonfire-night was going to be the best yet. About three days before Bonfire-night, I think it was late afternoon still light, I had just got home from School, there was a knock at the door, it was a Man in a Mac with a bloody great suitcase, he said hello Son, is your Mum in, with that I shouted to Mum that there was a Man at the door asking for you. I scurried of back into the bedroom to mess around with my Brother David, a school Boy now, he had started School in the September, I can remember telling him, there was a Man at the door with a massive suitcase.

After what seemed like eternity, Mum called, and told us the Mans name was John, and that he would be staying for Tea, little did any of us know, that his tea, would last for twelve years, more of that later, anyway we had no idea who this John was, but we thought he was a nice Man, but it seemed strange Mum sitting around the table with us, and this Man, at ease, laughing and joking. All Mum would tell us was he is a friend of your Fathers and he will be staying for a while. After tea, the Man was shown to his room, he had the spare room as David and I used to share.

Once he had unpacked he brought this suitcase back into the kitchen, which was the main room of the house, it was always warm because that is where the fire was. He put the suitcase on the table, John, soon to be nicknamed (Johnny Boy), called to David and myself, and said something like have you got any fireworks, we said yes, and with that he lifted the suitcase lid and said, here is some more. We couldn't begin to explain how happy we were, the suitcase was full of fireworks of all types, at that moment we didn't care who he was, and all we wanted to do was tell our mates. That Bonfire-night was without doubt the best we ever had, and the morning after was the best we ever had too.

I'm not sure how long it was before Mum told us who Johnny Boy really was, it turned out he was our Dad's Brother and that he had come down to try and sort thing out, yea-right, he was Dad's Brother, but still yea-right.

Just before Johnny Boy arrived we had moved to another Hut, it was just next door, no 12 we would all eventually be re-housed into proper houses, but it wasn't our turn quite yet, strangely enough it was the posh end that got the first choice of houses, we were moved to another hut so they could keep those that remained there closer together, that way they could demolish the huts much easier, which made sense.

We didn't mind moving to the new Hut, because although it was only next-door it was still an adventure.

This place had steps going down to the only door of the house, at the bottom of the steps was an Outhouse/junk room, I remember a game us Lads used to play, and OMG how dangerous was it, there was a light switch, the old brown bakelite type, the actual switch cover was bear to the elements, and somewhere, I can't quite remember, whether we were told you could do this, or just something we did by accident, anyway, we would get three four or five kids, to all hold hands, the one at the front would put a rod or something metal on the switch, the electricity would go through all the of us and the Kid at the end would get a hell of a shock, we would all change places until we had all got a mighty jolt, and sometimes we would form a circle so everyone got a jolt, dear oh bloody dear how foolish was that. Mum of course went ballistic when she discovered what we were doing, and very soon got the council to repair it.

Mum received a letter from the Council informing her that we have a date for moving, it was to be the following

August which was just after my eighth birthday, this was sometime, infact 10 months away, it was something to look forward to. To be honest David and myself loved living in Tin Town, we would have stayed there forever.

We never saw much of Johnny Boy, he used to work away and come back every now and again, and although we still didn't understand why he was around it didn't seem to bother us. We were far too busy living in our own little worlds, we sill had Christmas, spring and summer to enjoy, before we moved. I mentioned the Oliver's earlier, they were a strange family, and although George was our bodge hero, we really only got involved with him in the bodge racing season, which didn't seem to bother him or us, his Mum Mrs Oliver's was a little Lady with a contorted face, I wondered why she looked like that, probably a stroke, Mr Oliver (known as slasher) never lived with the family, we used to see him once a week, when he came to visit his children, the first time we saw him we all thought he was a tramp, and I suppose thinking about it now, he probably was.

When he came to visit he would do the same thing every time, Tin Town ran parallel with the main Cranbrook to Hastings road, we were quite high up, so we looked down onto the main road, Slasher would wedge himself in the bank the other side of the road, we were terrified of him but at the same time he fascinated us, he was a bit like a wild animal or something you were afraid of. The bank leading down to the road opposite Slasher, had a hole in the hedge, the bank itself was worn away smooth, where we used slide down, so we could cross the road and shout abuse at him then run like buggery. The main reason to get brave enough was to get close to him to see his legs and feet, he always removed his socks and shoes, then rolled his trousers up, his legs and feet were black, we thought it was because he never washed, which he probably didn't, but I'm sure now it was also to do with bad circulation, he would come to Tin Town every week, but he never saw his Kids because Mrs Oliver wouldn't let them. Then all of a sudden, we never saw Slasher again, he had probably passed away.

Tin Town was rapidly becoming a ghost Town, families seem to be moving out on a weekly basis, and every time a family left the rest of us if we were around, would all stand together and wave goodbye. It turned out we were the last leave.

David and I spent our final months kicking our heels, most of the kids were long gone, and instead of wanting to stay here forever, we now couldn't wait to move. The Bodge race never happened, the camp on the hillside was still there, which tended to be our most popular place to mess around.

Mum and Johnny Boy were busy packing; we were only moving about half a mile further up the road, a little village called Hartley, our address was No 3 Henniker Cottages. We couldn't wait.

Chapter 2.
No 3 Henniker Cottages.

It was early August 1953, moving day, obviously David and myself, never had a clue on the pitfalls of moving, we didn't know that moving was very stressful, and somehow they had to get all our furniture and belongings from Tin Town to Henniker Cotts, we still don't know to this day how everything got there, probably didn't, I think we walked up to Henniker with our Mum, and she left us there whilst Her and Johnny Boy did the move, the house was smaller than we thought, but it had an upstairs, we've never had an upstairs.

The access to upstairs was via a door from the kitchen, there were three bedrooms, biggest at the back with another double and single to the front, it also had a trap hatch to the loft, which will make some interesting reading a bit later on, back downstairs to the kitchen, located at the back with a door to the rear, the kitchen was of good size and over to one side was the bath fully visable at all times, there was just enough room to get a table in, we also a cupboard under the stairs, through a door leading to the front of the house, this was a sizable room with a fireplace it was our living room.

Outside, the front garden was of good size with a high hedge by the road, I got to know this hedge quite well as I got older, a path ran the whole length of the six cottages, with a further path teeing of to each dwellings, the path ran down the side of the house, halfway down the side of the house was the coal hole, built into the side of the house, the rear garden was extremely long and quite narrow, the cottages all backed onto fields, David and I were keen to explore these wide and open spaces as soon as we could, about twenty feet from the back door was a brick Outhouse, first part of the Outhouse was for storage etc, at the end was a door, we opened it to find a flush toilet, we never had this sort of luxury at Tin Town, and a Bath in the kitchen, ok today this seems awful but to us pure luxury. At Tin Town our bath was a galvanised affair in front of the fire, we knew we were going to like living here, the downside of things was we had to find new mates fast.

Johnny Boy by this time had got his feet under the table, and was sharing Mums bed, it meant nothing to us, and quite quickly he started to rule the roost, and his dark side began to raise its ugly head. We understand he used to work on the Shipyards in Birkenhead, so he was pretty useful with his hands.

At this moment in time he was renting a small building from the local garage in Gills Green, nr Hawkhurst, which was the next village along the A229, it was just a couple of miles further up the road, he used to do welding repairs and spraying, and when he came home from work he was absolutely filthy, god knows how he got that dirty, mind you he never wore overalls, and god help us if the bath wasn't full of hot water when he got home, to do this chore was a major operation, no hot water from taps, so everything had to be boiled in saucepans, very often he used to go directly to the pub on his way home, so everything went cold, we would never know what sort of mood he was in till he came through the door.

Opposite Henniker was Hartley House, Initially it was a Work House, then it became a Care Home for the Elderly, it wasn't long before, Mum got a job over there as a Registered Nurse, the regular wage was a god send, as Johnny Boy's contribution towards the household was very sporadic and quite often non existent, his work pattern was never a regular one, sometimes he would stay in bed until midday, then go to work until midnight, there were always blokes knocking on our door looking for him.

Our next door neighbours were the Fevers, Jean was married to Ron Fever, he was a very small timid chap, I think he was a window cleaner, Jean was short and dumpy, with very thin hair, and down the bottom of the garden was a very large wooden building, which intrigued David and me, we soon found out what it was, the rear gardens between the house and outhouses were divided by an hedge, next to the Fevers side of the hedge was a very large metal water tank, it must have been ten feet long by three feet wide by four feet deep, one day we heard someone putting something into or taking something out of the tank, on this occasion they were taking something out, we couldn't quite see what it was, but could just about catch the odd glimpse of the person that was doing the job. They made their way down towards the large wooden building at the bottom of the garden. We had to see who it was, and to our amazement it was a man that seemed to walk in a somewhat strange manner, he had his head tilted almost skywards, he had a bundle of canes under his arm, we suddenly realised the Man was Blind, we had never seen a Blind Person before.

To us it was quite frightening, actually seeing someone blind, we said hello to him, he turned his head towards us but still tilted skywards, and replied you must be the our new neighbours, we said yes we were, after a few words he asked us if we would like to have a look in the building to see what he did, we of course said yes, so we ran out to the front, along the path then down the path that led us to the Fevers back garden, as we got to the back of their house, we heard the door open, it was Jean Fever, she asked us what we were doing there, I said we were talking to a blind man and he said we could go and have a look in his big shed, with that she escorted us to the bottom of their garden, opened the door and said, Ted I have a couple of Boys from next door, you said could come and have a look, he said come in Boys, we slowly made our way in, there was another Man in there as well, his name was Albert, he was Ted's brother, and to our amazement he was blind too, we stayed for quite a while, they told us all sorts of tales, needless to say they were basket weavers. I was very interested and gob smacked at how they could do such things, without being able to see, they even let us have a go, over the following years we would pop and see them quite a bit, we found out that Ron was their Brother, the only one not to loose his sight, I believe one was born blind and the other went blind, when he was young, thinking about it now the Fevers were the only ones at Henniker that never got any grief from us, I think deep down we were frightened of them, because they were different.

Henniker Cottages

Henniker Cottages comprised of 6 dwellings, 3 pairs of Cottages, we were no 3, at number 2 lived the Normans, they were a very old couple, Mr Norman or Daddy Norman as we called him, was always in the garden tending to his large selection of vegetables, he had a chicken run at the bottom of his garden, quite often, we would nip into the run and pinch the odd egg, Mum would have gone ballistic if she new. Then there was Mrs Norman or Cider Annie as we called her, apparently she loved cider and once a week she would be seen with her shopping trolley hobbling off to the Railway Tavern, it was the only pub in Hartley, which was about half a mile further up the road, quite a big pub, and always busy, it was chocker block at weekends, and during the hop picking season it was fantastic, all the hoppers from London, drinking and singing, and generally having a good time, amazing compared with today, a tiny village with a full pub?, mmm not anymore, the R/Tavern sat on the main road opposite a T junction which lead down to Cranbrook Railway Station, and at the time steam trains were still running. With Daddy Norman and Cider Annie lived a young boy, his name was Roy Norman, he was their Grandson, Roy was very backward, and would always have a mental age of an eight year old, they loved that little Lad, his parents didn't want him, poor devil, we never really saw much of the Normans, only saw Cider Annie on her weekly trip to the Pub, Roy hardly ever, although we used to hear him playing in the back yard, but it was difficult to see him as the top end of their garden was surrounded by very tall firs trees, I suppose we saw Daddy Norman more than the others, seeing him was about it, he very rarely spoke, but that suited us, when he had his back turned we would pull faces at him, that's the sort of little sods we were.

In number one live the Roots, nicknamed Mummy and Daddy Roots, and a son, to be honest we never new much about them, apart from the fact he was famous for his bonfires, smoking the rest of us out.

At number five were the Westerns, Joe Western, know as Smokey Joe, because he was a fireman in the war, he was also a dispatch rider, there is a picture in the Cranbrook museum of Joe posing on his motor bike in his uniform. Joe had that tobacco smell about him, it was because he smoked very strong roll ups, his wife Amy was a biggish Lady, and had these funny eyes, IE one looking to the left the other looking to the right, very strange, Joe was twenty years older than Amy. They had four girls and two boys, starting with the oldest was, June, Ellen, Bobby, Philip, Avril and Christine, a lot for a very small three up and two down with the bath in the kitchen, it wasn't too long before we became friends with the westerns, more of that later.

At number six was the Leonard's, who were completely different to the rest of us, there was Mr and Mrs Leonard, quite old, well into their seventies, daughter Marge, a very thin woman, one that always looked posh, oh and there was their little dog called Tiny, bloody thing, used to yap day and night. Their house and garden compared to the rest, apart from the Fevers, was immaculate, god knows what they thought when us lot moved in!

I cannot remember to much about the first few months at Henniker, apart from the fact Johnny Boy's temper, he used to have a smash ups, as we called them, on a regular basis, these smash ups, got more and more frequent, he would blow his top for the smallest reason, such as, on one occasion when we were having dinner, David pinched an extra potatoes from the dish, with that Johnny Boy turned the table over, everything went all over the place, then he would say, as he always did after a smash up, now clean that lot up, we legged it and got lost until we thought it was calm enough to go home, when we get back it was like it always was, Mum had cleaned everything up, Johnny Boy had either gone up the pub, or was in the front room very quiet, and we knew not to venture into that room, as he could and has quite often did, flare up again, these smash ups went on for quite a number of years, until we got old enough to stand against him.

Mum was to work at the Home (Hartley House as it was known) until we left Henniker Cottages some ten years later, one week she worked from 9am to 4-30pm the following week she did 1pm to 9-30pm. Hartley House looked like an old fashioned Hospital. With its stone walls and big arched entrance, it looked quite grand but inside it was the typical old hospital, but more like the Workhouse, it was originally built for. While mum was at work, during the holidays we would very often creep over the road to the Home, and have fun in the front gardens that were laid out to perfection, lawns and flower beds, with fir trees and benches scattered about, for the more able bodied residence to sit and have a natter, or just be on their own to while away the day, as I said we would have loads of fun hiding up trees and in bushes, making silly noises to frighten the residence, that was until the gardener found out, he reported it, Mum got a rollicking, we got a thick ear, and needless to say, we never went there again.

Hartley House

Not to worry we had plenty of options up our sleeves. One option was at the bottom of our garden; it was Henniker, a very large field that seemed to go on forever. Nothing was ever grown in it, the farmer would cut the grass maybe once a year, and that was it, right down the bottom of the field, was Henniker Woods, and it had a big pond which was to give us loads of fun over the coming years.

Henniker field was split in half by a ditch, that started at the top and went all the way into the woods, it was dead straight, and we soon found out, it was made by a German Doodle Bug, a pilot less craft that was launched from Germany, with just enough fuel to reach London, very often they never made it and crashed all over the south of England. All very exciting stuff for an eight year old to be told, I think it was one of Albert Fevers stories. The other half of the field which was to the left didn't really interest us much, apart from the conker season, as it had two great big conker trees, Oh it was also another way to go to Cranbrook and miss having to walk along

27

the main road as much, once you reached the far top left hand corner of this field, there was a grass path that runs alongside Parkers house, leading you back onto the main road, at the top of Parkers hill, as we called it, Mr Parker had a small shop that sold fresh bread, fruit and vegetables, along with a variety of tinned produce, he also sold Smiths crisps, the one with the twist of salt, If I'm correct it was about that time when another brand of crisps came on the market, and I can't think for the love of me what they were called, but if I do I will certainly include it somewhere, all I do know, is before too long there were all sorts of brands and flavours, until then it was Plain or Salt and Vinegar. By Smiths

Our first Summer Holidays at No 3 Henniker Cottages, was fast approaching. David and I couldn't wait, in those days the summers all seemed to be hot, with one or two massive thunder storms, the sky very often would go so black it was like night, I remember seeing a tree at the bottom of Henniker field, being split in two, by bolt lightning, and the hail stones, it wasn't uncommon to see them on the ground as big as marbles.

By that time we had made friends with Barry Nash, a lad that lived a few houses down, he lived in number 2 Pleasant View, which was a very large, and we thought posh ground floor two bedroom flat, his Mum was and still is a lovely person, and to this day, we keep in touch by sending birthday and Christmas cards with a few word of news, sadly Mr Nash died quite a few years ago, he only had one eye, he used to work for the electricity board, and the story goes, he was up a electricity pole when a wire, flashed over his eye, he unfortunately lost his site in that eye, in those days, they never seemed to be able to perfect the likeness to the good eye, so it really did look quite odd. Mrs Nash was, so house proud, and I can remember the tiled floors were so clean and shiny; they had this entrance hall that went from the front door all the way down to the kitchen, fantastic for sliding on. We used to love going there for tea they seemed to have all the good stuff, like cakes, and pies, and also I suppose the main reason was because, they had a television, we would watch programmes like the Lone Ranger, the Cisco Kid, lots of Westerns. And some fifty years later Mrs Nash still lives at number 2 Pleasant View. When I left School my first job was as a butchers Boy, and it was for Mrs Nash's Dad Horace, more of that later on.

Mum used to have quite a number of visitors; there was Eric Wheatley, the Man from the Pru! He was always popping in, and I think it wasn't always for the insurance money, I thought he was a bit of a sleaze ball, never really liked him, there used to be all sorts of rumours flying about, I was far too young to understand or care, but yes I do recall quite a bit of chemistry going on between them, then there was Jimmy Miller from Hawkhurst, a furniture removal Man, I quite liked him, when I was a bit older Mum would take me to the Bull at Rolvenden, to watch him play in the Pub Darts Team, he was pretty good, and good fun, I worked for him a few years later, just the one day, and never again, he used to get so up tight, he would eff and blind at the workforce, to watch this, don't knock that etc, he was a bloody nightmare to work for.

Summer here so what do we do? Me David, Barry Nash, and a new found mate of David's called Bunyan had big plans!

As you hop over our fence at the bottom of the garden there is a small copse that runs along the field on the left hand side, we nick-named it Nash's Wood, simply because it was owned by a miserable old sod called Mr Nash, nothing whatsoever to do with Barry Nash, just a coincidence, Mr Nash was a Fish Monger, he delivered fish to people around and about, we used to call him fishy Nash.

Our summer plan was to go into his wood and use it as a base, when we tried to enter the wood we couldn't, due to it being overgrown with brambles, this did not deter us, we soon got to work, within a few days made good headway and before too long we were well into his wood, when we decided it was deep enough into Fishy Nash's Wood. It was phase two, which was to make a clearing, this required the chopping down of several trees, some I remember quite tall, god knows how, but we managed to chop the trees down without Fishy Nash knowing, he should have done, as his bungalow's garden backed onto his wood not far from where we were, our clearing was finished, the final phase was to dig two big holes, they must have been four feet deep by at least four feet round, these holes were about eight feet apart, once dug we then tunnelled from one to the other, thinking about it now, it was bloody dangerous, but we had no idea about the danger aspects, we were having a great time, the ground was very hard so I expect that was in our favour, regarding them caving in, if they had of done, we could have been killed, these tunnels took for ever but we got there, and when we met in the middle, as we were digging from both tunnels and it was absolutely fantastic, we were quite a bit out with our calculations so it wasn't a direct hit we ended up having bit of a curve in the middle, our camp was complete apart from fitting it out with bits and bobs, such as pots and pans, a couple of water carriers, some old blankets etc, we even covered the tops of the holes with wood from the trees we chopped down.

Us lads spent most of the summer hols there, we were sure, no one ever knew where we were, we used to pinch a bit tea, the odd slice of bread, light a fire, make tea in a Billy can, always put a couple of thin pieces of wood in the water to take the smokiness away, something I learnt when we were hop picking, we would also do some toast, which was always burnt to a crisp, but we thought it was great.

Unfortunately it was short lived, towards the end of the Summer Hols, there was a mother of all thunder storms with torrential rain, it must have poured for 3 days or more, when the weather cleared up, we went down to our beloved camp, only to find it had filled up with water and the tunnel collapsed we were devastated, so we decided to move onto other things.

However this wasn't the end of the camp in Fishy Nash's Wood, one day we decided to walk down to Cranbrook Railway Station, which we very often did, as it was fun to see the Trains coming into the Station, with all the steam coming from almost every part of the engine, and there was a tunnel not far down the line, we would lean over the top and watch the train go into the tunnel, quite often we would get engulfed in all the smoke and steam, it was great, we would also spend hours on the banks that led down to the lines, and find all sorts of things to do, of course there was always a camp involved. Anyway on this particular day when we thought we should make our way home, as we got almost to the end of the approach road to the Station, Fishy Nash was driving his fish van towards us, we didn't think too much about it, but he stopped pretty quick and before we had time to leg it, he was out of his van, and collared us, obviously we were interrogated about his wood and the trees being chopped down, plus the holes in the ground, we never had a leg to stand on, and I can remember his last words to this very day, he said do you know what," you should be going up the steps mean," we had no idea, he said it means you could go to prison for what you have done, with that he said, don't you ever do this again, and drove off, we never heard another thing, mind you we were all shitting ourselves for a few days, wondering if he was going to tell our parents, but thankfully it all blew over.

So another drama out of the way and it was soon to be the end of the holiday, school was looming up. We were still at the Cranbrook Primary School, which meant a bus ride, there were no school buses, so it was public transport for us, thankfully there was a bus stop about five hundred yards down the road, the fare was the grand sum of one penny, doesn't seem a lot, but it was very difficult for mum to find the fare every day, so sometimes we would have to walk, it was about a mile and a half, which was a long way for David seven and myself just nine. The bus stop was outside the Chapman's house, Mrs Chapman was a teacher at the girls school, they had a Son who we made friends with, and every now and again we were invited to tea, it was a big house with a big garden, and we always felt uncomfortable because of it's poshness, don't know why we were always welcomed and never once did they say anything that might makes us feel that way.

On the opposite side of the road from the bus stop, was a large house, it had the look of a Swiss Cottage, all in white weather board, with a veranda which went the whole length of the front of the house the sort of place you would expect to see a Grandma and Grandpa sitting enjoying the day. In fact at that particular time, the actor James Hater owned it. He also went on to be known for his advert for Mr Kippling; with the phrase "He made exceedingly good cakes". He was always polite when we saw him, which was quite a lot, because he used walk past Henniker Cottages, on his way to the Railway Tavern, apparently he was quite a character.

The Swiss Cottage

The approach to Hartley from Cranbrook is by the A229 Maidstone to Hastings road, as you leave Cranbrook it's a gentle clime all the way to the Memorial, at that point the road levels off for about a quarter of a mile, past Goddard's Green Cottages on your left, then past Tin Town, whats left of it on your right. As you leave Tin Town the A229 rises steeply but only for about three to four hundred yards then it levels off again, at the top is Parkers, with the rough pathway leading to Henniker field, and the woods, to the left, the was lined with big trees and on a wet and windy night the rustling and creaking of the trees made it very eerie indeed, we would run like buggery when it was dark.

Cranbrook actually had it's own Cinema, called the Regal, we would go to the sat morning kids films, the one that sticks in my mind is Flash Gordon, it used to frighten the life out of us, sometimes we didn't have the money for both David and myself, not to worry, it was dead easy to get one or two in, the toilets were to the right of the screen, and as you went through the first door, to get to the loo, there was a fire door on the right, which opened out onto the rear of the Cinema, David would be waiting for the door to open so he could nip in, nobody ever twigged what we up to.

The Regal Cinema

Some Saturdays whilst David and I went to the pictures, Johnny Boy would go to the Cranbrook Tip, he was a right scavenger, and looked like a Tramp, he would always take an old pram to put any bits in, he was into bits and pieces, for radios and television, television hadn't been about long, Johnny Boy could make something out of nothing, I remember a contraption he put together, that when the alarm clock went off, it would put the radio on, he also made a potato peeler, that was basically a small drum that he punched holes in, pushing the jagged edges into the inside of the drum, he then put a handle on the drum, the theory being, you put some spuds in the drum, turn the handle, which was supposed to peel the spud, all it did was to rip the potato to bits, the more you turned the smaller the spud got, it never really worked. All the stuff he found at the tip would be stored in the loft via the trap hatch which was located on the stairs landing, it wasn't long before he had it boarded out to make a floor, he then made a work bench, installed electric lights and plugs. Christ knows how much rubbish he had up there, I'm surprised the ceiling never caved in, we would pop up there when he was out to have a look, naturally he found out, went bonkers, then fitted a padlock, so that was that. His violent temper, on many occasions, would raise its ugly head, for example, if we were noisy in bed, he would tear up the stairs, and go ballistic, it was always me that got the brunt of it, because he was so horrible, I would jump out of the bedroom window, David would throw me a blanket and pillow, and I would sleep under the hedge in the front garden until morning, sometimes it was bloody freezing.

Just before the summer hols ended, I can remember a couple of Coppers knocking on the door, there was only Johnny Boy and myself at home, David was out messing around with one of his new found mates. The Cops came in, had a chat with Johnny Boy, then went around the house, it seemed they were looking for something, I remember Johnny Boy saying, can I leave a note with the Boy, to give to his Mum, so she knows where I am, Johnny Boy scribbled on a bit of paper, he then gave it to me and staring quite strange, as if he was trying to tell me something, he put the note in my pocket making quite a thing about it, pushing it hard into my pocket and looking at me in that strange way, with that he went off with the police, although I didn't realise then, it was obvious they had arrested him, and taken him to the Cops shop. Being curious I put a hand in my pocket and pulled out the piece of paper, along with a key, it simply said, this key is for the loft, behind the water tank are two boxes with brass dials, fittings and things, I want you to get them away from the house, don't mind what you do but get rid of them. My heart started pumping, I think I was excited, and frightened all at the same time, so up in the Loft I went, this time, with full permission, I followed the instructions in his note, found the boxes, it was a good job I knew where the light was, in the boxes were all sorts of strange looking things, I didn't have a clue what they were, just knew I had to get rid of them, first task was to get these items out of the loft, which for a nine year old, and only just nine at that, my Birthday was on the 14th July. I can't quite remember how I did it, but I must have managed somehow, I can recall, that I decided to put them into the Outhouse, in readiness to sling them in Henniker Pond. It was a good job that Johnny Boy was taken away by the Coppers, not long after breakfast, as it was about to be a long long day for a nine year old. It was quite a trip on it's own to Henniker Pond, without having to lug all this stuff, I lost count of the amount of journeys it took, and I was so happy when the last run was done.

Mission completed, and I was quite chuffed with myself, and was looking forward to telling Johnny Boy, how well I had done, it seemed like eternity before he came home, but when he eventually arrived I couldn't contain myself, this was a big moment for me, with Johnny Boy, he never

ever gave us a pat on the back, praised us or said well done, I was looking forward seeing his reaction.

He said did you get rid of the stuff? Yes I replied, he asked where I put them, I explained that I had taken them to Henniker Pond, now this was when everything went pear shaped, he told me to go and bring them back, I informed him that I had thrown them in the pond, he went berserk, and gave me such a hiding, I was devastated, thinking what a great job I had done, and that I had worked so hard that day, and all he could do was go ballistic, the selfish sod, that was the last time I would do anything to get him out of trouble again.

Although back to school was beckoning, I knew that at least I had a few extra days, due to Hop picking, and this time it was going to be a bit of a walk to Enfield's Farm, but not to worry, the other thing that I can recall about that time of the year, was all the people that used to travel from London, they would arrive in droves and treat Hop Picking as their holiday, they lived in rows of brick huts, that were on the Hop Farms and built by the Farmers, we called them Hopper Huts. The Londoners always seemed a jolly lot, it wasn't just Mum, Dad, and the Kids that came, it was the entire family, Grandma. Grandad, even the pets, I've seen Parrots, Budgies, all sorts, there would always be a fire going with the regulation Billy Can outside the huts, plus a couple of sticks of wood, you would see them in the evening all together the Men having a few beers, whilst the Kids were playing, the woman were cooking and washing. What was upsetting was the fact they were treated like undesirables we always knew when they were on there way as all the shops would put up chicken wire fences along the counters and move everything back behind, it so it never got stolen, Our nearest shop was the Tollhouse Stores, where I used to go to get Mum's 5 tipped woodbines, it was the tiniest of shops, and it sat what appeared to be in the middle of the road, imagine the tip of an arrow, and living in the very tip with a road brushing by either side, that's what it was like. The shop was flanked one side by the A229 on its left, with the Goudhurst road slipping off from the A229 to it's right, Tollhouse Stores was literally right beside the road, they did very well out of the London Hop Pickers, as far as I can remember not one of them ever complained about being treated this way, or maybe they thought the fences were always there, and that was what it was like in the Countryside! I would dread to think what would happen if it was like that today.

Yes I was looking forward to my half a bin, and also seeing the antics of Gary Blanch, nicknamed Lunchy, a tall scruffy fellow with a long unruly beard, always stripped to the waist, he was the Man, that used to drive the tractor and trailer twice a day to the Hop Fields, then measure the hops with a bushel basket, put them into sacks, then load them on the trailer, which was taken back to the farm for stacking, before they were put into the hop kilns for drying and pressing, they were then put into large sacks, could hop pokes (I think). He was a right charmer with the Ladies, they loved him, I remember one day he was showing off and larking about, he fell off the trailer and broke his arm, he was back to work the very next day in plaster, still driving the tractor, still measuring the hops, still charming the Ladies, just like George Oliver (the bodge king) he was our hero as well, for a few weeks a year.

On our way home from Hop picking, Mum would very often stop to have a chat with the Men and Woman, that were Hay making in one of the fields next to the Goddard's Green Cottages, I can remember the Men cutting the hay, whilst the Woman bundled it up, putting it into stacks, ready to be collected by the tractor and trailer, I'm not sure quite who the people were, working in the hay field, I have an inkling it was Mums Brother, my Uncle Ron, maybe My Grandad (Mums Dad) and the rest of them I really don't know, it's just that this field next to Goddard's Green Cottages, is a memory of a calm Summers evening, with people laughing and joking, money can't buy that, and I always think about it. Every time I passed by, even today.

Goddards Green Cottages, how they are today. The field is to the right.

One evening when we had just got home from Hopping, there was a knock on the front door, a smart Man was at the door, it was obvious, Mum knew who he was, she asked him in, they had a cup of tea and a chat, they seemed quite friendly, said their goodbyes, he then left, when he was gone, I said to Mum, that was my Dad wasn't it? She said yes it was, I must admit I was quite upset that he never even spoke to me, and to be honest I was hoping that he may drop in again quite soon, this was on my mind for quite a while, but in the end I put it out of my mind, and I suppose that is why, I really am not bothered any more.

Over the past few years Johnny Boy, had without doubt stamped his mark on things, including the fathering of 2 boys and a Girl with Mum, Christopher, Peter and a girl named Eileen, this put pressure on Mum, trying to work and look after us lot was quite a handful, she had to find someone to look after the youngest three, thankfully Mrs Giles, just up the road in Campian Crescent, offered to look after them.

If Mum was at work I had to take them up to Mrs Giles, then collect them later on in the day, sometimes I even had to change their nappies, a right performance for a ten year old, and bearing in mind, it wasn't the easy peasy ones you get today, these were just square pieces of towelling, that had to be folded in a certain way, then fixed with big safety pins, not the sort of job to place in the hands of a ten year old, but what else could Mum have done? Christopher and Peter turned out to be the brainy ones, Chris went to Tunbridge Wells Technical College looking very smart in his dark blazer white shirt, tie and long grey trousers,

Peter had his Secondary Education In London, when we all moved there, more of this later.

Looking after my Brothers and Sister continued for quite sometime, we had to fit our own leisure activity in, as and when, I can never recall Johnny Boy changing a nappy, or taken them to Mrs Giles, thinking about it, he was a lazy sod, he only did what suited him.

Which was rolling out of bed halfway through the day, either going to his workshop, or down the pub, where he would play the piano to pay for his drinks, infact he was very good at tickling the ivories, and over the following years he built up quite a reputation, he used to play almost every Saturday night at some Pub or other.

I remember what a fiasco it sometimes was as Johnny Boy preened himself on a Saturday in readiness to go out, on one occasion in particular, we had done all the usual things including filling his bath up, Etc Etc. Whilst he had his bath we were banished to the front room, all seemed fine, when all of a sudden there was an almighty scream from the kitchen, it was Johnny Boy calling me, I entered the kitchen to see him standing with his back to me crouched over hiding his bits and pieces, he said the bloody water is going out of the bath, put the plug in, the plug was a flannel which we pushed up the waste pipe on the outside of the house, god knows why it was like that, but that's how he wanted it, so outside I went trying to push this bloody flannel back up the pipe against the tide as it were, he was shouting and screaming, but he could do sod all about it standing in that bath, I can still recall seeing his naked body for the first time, he was quite white and skinny, apart from his neck and the bottom of his arms which were red and grained with what seemed like oil, his body had loads of boils on it, when he went off to the pub piano playing, we spent the rest of that evening laughing until we couldn't laugh anymore.

I think deep down Mum was at her happiest when Johnny Boy wasn't around; if there was any magic between them it was long gone. Plus we Kids were much happier as well, although he would eventually leave, that moment was a long - long way off.

Chapter 3.
Swattenden School for Boys

I can't remember much about the remaining couple of years at Cranbrook Primary School, it was just a matter of going there and going home, I wasn't unhappy at school, it just didn't seem that important to me, as far as I know I was a bright lad but one that didn't really try enough, apparently I passed the eleven plus, which meant I qualified to go to Cranbrook Grammar School, which was, and still is a very well known establishment, pupils pay a fortune to go there now, Mum just couldn't afford to send me there, to be quite honest I didn't want to go anyway, I wanted to be with my mates at Swatttenden School for Boys.

"Summer of 1956." The end of my time at Cranbrook Primary School. Again I do not remember anything about what happened on those final days, it was probably because I was looking forward to going to Swattended the Big School.

We spent the summer holidays doing the usual things, plus David and myself were off to stay with our Auntie Elsie,

Mums Sister, they lived just outside Tenterden, which is a lovely Town and still the same to this day, apart from the traffic of course, it has one Street that is almost dead straight, lined in Poplar Trees, back then there were loads of Pubs and a Cinema, bigger than the one at Cranbrook, we would go to see the latest films when we got a bit older, on the 97 Bus, which was always good fun, especially when there was a few of us, mind you the Bus Conductor didn't take that view, Tenterden was a Town about seven miles away, it is situated between Rolvenden and Ashford, we were going to stay with Auntie Elsie for a few days, to give Mum a well earned rest, although she still had Chris, Peter and Eileen to look after.

We would always go and stay about once a year, which David and myself really looked forward to, we loved Auntie Elsie's the best, she was married to Jim, not tall, but a powerful looking Man, His arms were big with enormous muscles, Uncle Jim worked on the local farm so I suppose that is why he was so fit and strong.

They lived in a big old house that was split into two dwellings, which was owned by the Council, it's now a private house that has been renovated, it sits right at the foot of an open valley of fields giving one of the most beautiful views around, the road from Cranbrook to Tenterden, runs alongside the front of the House, which isn't a problem, as the House lies well back, the road is a B road, and snakes its way up the valley, until it disappeared at the top, joining the main Tenterden to Rye and Hastings road, halfway up the valley was a level crossing, and if I remember correctly, there were two trains a day, one quite early and the other about tea time, we loved watching the train puffing their way across the middle of the valley, Jim and Elsie's flat was on the ground floor, the rear garden was big and seemed to loose itself into the field, to the left hand side of the rear garden as you came out of the house, was a brick wall, it ran the whole length of the field, and this was where all the human waste from the chemical toilets were emptied, it just looked like a thick black stream, it had a strange smell about it but to be honest nothing that we found to be unbearable. Towards the end of the garden were sheds of all sizes, some were still being used to store garden tools, others to keep fertilizer and the rest were simply filled with all sorts of rubbish, to us it was paradise, we would spend hours just moving things about, making out we were workers, it's amazing how a couple of kids can just loose themselves for an afternoon.

Auntie Elsie's, certainly wasn't like this way back then.

One of the Trains crossing the valley

As teatime beckoned Auntie Elsie would call out to us, by then we were starving, she was very house proud, so we had to remove our boots, tea was great, there was this very long table in the kitchen, that was propped up at one corner, as the floor was of brick, and not level, Auntie Elsie would always have plenty of food to fill the table, big thick door steps of bread, maybe a bowl of soup to dip our bread in, and always some cakes or sausage rolls.

As night drew in, it was time to light the lamps, something Uncle Jim would do, at night it was such a magical place, the soft lighting from the lamps, and the smell of the paraffin burning away on the lamp wicks, the radio would always be on, we would tell Uncle Jim and Auntie Elsie what we had been up to, leaving out of course anything we considered may get us into trouble. Yes we enjoyed our stays at Uncle Jims and Elsie's.

It was always a sad occasion when we had to go home, but it was great to see Mum, and tell her everything, well nearly everything we had been up to, I think we always went to our Aunties in the first or second week of the summer holiday, we certainly wasn't looking forward to seeing Johnny Boy, but couldn't wait to tell Chris, Peter and Eileen what we had been up to, with a bit of exaggeration, of course. The summer holidays seemed to fly by; it was probably because I was worrying about going to the Big School. Swattenden was about 2 miles away from Henniker, and with no school bus or public transport if you lived that close, you had to find your own way there, Swattenden was quite a walk, as you went out of our front gate, turn left, walk for about a quarter of a mile, then turn left down Swattenden Lane, it is quite a narrow lane which twists and turns all the way, going past a couple of ponds, first being the Haunted, I caught a pound and an half Roach there, on just a daisy once, past the Council yard, Mr Trower was the boss, I remember going out with one of his Daughters, I think her name was Jean, I was only a little squirt of a lad, and she towered over me like an Amazon Warrior, then past Mears Farm, we used to go strawberry and blackcurrant picking, making ourselves ill by eating too many, then round a very sharp S bend, it had a pond on it's left, the Barn Pond, I actually taught myself to swim there, I remember swimming and catching my knee on something in the water, there was blood everywhere, when I got out of the pond I looked down to see one hell of a gash across my left knee, I had to have quite a few stitches in it, I still have a scare on my knee to this day, as you exit the S bend you pass the Barn Farm on your left, then the countryside opens up, as it opened up Swattenden

School could be clearly seen on the right hand side, after a few hundred yards there was this big sign at the entrance saying "Swattenden School for Boys" with a gatehouse on your right, our Science Teacher Mr George lived there with his wife and son Michael, sadly Michael was killed in a car accident a few years later, as you enter the school grounds, it's very impressive, with all the football and athletic fields on the left, all looking green and lush, I was excited, there is a long road from the main road to the School itself, the school buildings are directly in front of you, looking just like a stately home, this was the heart of the School, all the other buildings were long single story, each building was allocated to a certain subject, there were Woodwork and Metalwork buildings, which joined each other. Opposite these was the Science building, Mr George's domain. Then halfway up the approach road to the School was the History building, Mr Chadwick was the Teacher, he lived in that Swiss type house in Hartley, before the Actor James Hayter, after Swattenden, the lane continues twisting, uphill and down dale, to the next Village called Benenden, where Princess Anne went to School, The Benenden School for Girls.

It was just a few days away before I started my new school, Mum decided it was too far for me to walk, so she promised me a bike, I've never been on a bike, I was wondering where this bike was coming from, although I'm still a bit vague about that, I think it was Jimmy Miller, the Furniture Man, I remember this bike arriving, even in those days, this bike was so old fashioned, it was so big and clumsy looking, even the saddle seemed something from another age, it was far too large for my tiny backside, plus it had those bloody great springs under the seat, which would pinch my bear thighs, bearing in mind I was a Titch of a Lad, as I stood against it, the crossbar was level with my shoulder, I'm sure my face must have changed from elation to disappointment when I first clapped my eyes on this awful looking machine, I was sat on the bike, only to find the pedals were miles away from my feet, Jimmy put his arm round me and said not to worry, I will sort it for you, he came back the next day, he had fitted blocks to the pedals, I was aware that a lot of the kids had blocks fitted to their bikes, but nothing like this, I then had to learn how to ride the thing, I was lifted onto the bike, then given a helping push, after a few adjustments to the pedals I was well away in fact enjoying every minute of it, I found the best way to mount this great big ugly black machine was to put my right foot on the pedal scoot like buggery then hop my left leg over the saddle and hope for the best.

So the trial run was out of the way, Mum had got my uniform, although I was rather hoping for long trousers I had short ones, and I knew that I would be one of the very few that would be wearing short trousers. School was beckoning.

The big day had arrived, all the, "have you got this, have you done that", was over, it was just a matter of strapping my satchel somewhere to the bike, slinging my left leg over the saddle and making my way to the Swattenden School, I remember Mum coming out to the main road giving me a hug saying something daft in my ear and offering a helping push to get me away, I said no let me do it, after a wobbly start I was away.

It seemed to take no time at all, to get to the School, I remember arriving at the entrance, there was a Man standing there, he told me to get off my bike, this was something I hadn't put into the equation, I almost fell over trying to make a classy dismount, but the most embarrassing was to happen, a lot of the big kids were already there ready to pick on us new kids they sneered and laughed at me, because of my bike, I realised how stupid I looked, shoulders no higher than the crossbars, and the pedal blocks were so ridiculous. That was the first and last time I ever rode that bike to school. Until I got myself a decent bike, I chose to walk to School.

Now I was the ripe old age of Eleven and a bit, I decided to look for some sort of job, and I wanted a job so badly, it meant I could save up and buy myself a bike from Martins the local bike shop, I found out that he did a savings club for Lads that had a paper round, and were looking to buy a new or second hand Bike, It was easy really, just pop some money into him, he would mark it in your Club book, and once there was enough to buy the bike of your choice hey presto. So what sort of job do I look for? The obvious one was a paper round. In those days getting your Sunday, daily papers and magazines delivered through the letterbox was very popular, as was early morning milk, Cranbrook had three newsagents two in the High Street and one halfway along the Stone Street, it wasn't that easy getting a job as a paper Boy, you had to put your name down then wait for a vacancy, I put my name down with all three, I knew quite a few of the paper Boys so I kept my nose to the ground, hoping to get the news about a vacancy before anyone else, I would pop into the Newsagents at least once a week to see if there were any paper rounds coming available.

I'm not sure if it was my persistence, because before to long I was offered a job, from Lees in the Stone Street, it wasn't quite what I wanted, but it was a job, Mr Lee said I was just that little bit too young to have my own round, but he needed someone to work with the Man that delivered the papers in the Van, apparently it was a big round and he needed help, thinking about it now, it was probably the best paper round I ever had, being run around in a Van delivering papers and getting paid, fantastic, I was told by Mr Lee, all I had to do was be on time, work hard and be honest. I cannot remember the wage but I really didn't care, I had a job and my dream to buy myself a pushbike had begun. Until that day arrived I had to walk to the shop then home again, but quite soon the chap that I did the paper round with, decided to pick me up and drop me back home when the round was finished.

One of the Newsagent Shops I worked at, same Shop, different name.

I felt so good and grown up, I made sure that I popped some money into Martins every week as soon as I was paid, The bike shop was a gathering place for quite a few of us Lads, most of us, if not all of us were buying themselves a bike or exchanging the old one through the Club, so we all met there, just after we had been paid. Mr Martin was a really nice Bloke, he used to always wear one of those light brown working coats that maintenance people wore, his life was bikes, he was never without a spanner in his hand, his shop was like an Aladdin's Cave, and outside on the wide pavement Mr Martin would put a few second hand bikes, as you walked in he had a few brand new bikes on display, all shining away in there different colours, the walls were shelved and stacked out with all sorts of goodies, that could adorn your treasured bike. At the far end was a counter the full width of the shop, part of the counter would lift up to allow Mr Martin to get into the display area, the wall behind the counter was chocker block with screws, chains, bulbs, etc, etc, we all loved that shop. If Mr Martin wasn't that busy, you would see him outside his shop, passing the time of day with the locals, It took me eighteen months to get my bike, but the wait was worth it, as I had saved enough for a brand new one, I think it was a Raleigh, in bright red, I can still remember to this day, walking up to his shop to collect my bike, I got off the 97 bus that stopped at the bottom of the High Street outside the White Horse Pub, as I walked up towards Martins I can recall seeing my bike outside, waiting for me, I've never been more excited about anything, what a day. I could now bike to school with pride, and show off my new bike, the first few weeks I was terrified to get it scratched or damaged, we had a place to park our bikes at school, it was just the other side of the Science building, I used to keep an eye on it as much as I could, to make sure it was still ok, like most things the novelty went away, and although I loved that bike it soon became just a bike, but a bike with Street cred. Not like that other contraption. Now going to school all of a sudden, wasn't that bad after all.

I must admit to the fact, that I was enjoying going to Swattenden, much more than Cranbrook Primary, somehow I felt more grown up. I loved the sports and it was fair to say that I excelled in some, I was the fastest at 100 yards, I never got on with cross Country running, to me it seemed silly, in fact a couple of us when out on the run, would never actually do the run, it was probably something like a 5 mile run, we would hide up in an old packing shed in the entrance to the first field, just after we had run through the main part of Barn Farm, as we entered the field there was a shed, we always made sure we were in last position, so not to be seen by the other kids, we would then hide in the shed, usually playing five stones etc until the runners came back, then craftily tag on the back, I'm sure the teacher was suspicious of me always being last, as I seemed so competitive in other Sports, I went on to hold the pole vault record for the County Schools Championship, I can remember seeing a photo of myself in the window of the Kent and Sussex Newspaper shop, at Cranbrook I was clearing the bar to win, with the caption, it's not as easy as it looks, I would look in that window whenever I could.

Sadly once it was yesterday's news, I was not in the window anymore, so my bit of fame had gone. I was also the School Goalkeeper, even though I had great difficulty reaching the crossbar, I hated Cricket just found it boring, and still do to this very day.

I enjoyed most subjects, apart from geography, I was pretty good at mathematics english and science, woodwork and metalwork never really interested me, all I can ever remember of these subjects was, file or cut to the line, another reason could have been, was the fact that one of my class mates Derek Gurr, was a bit of a bully, quite big for his age, particularly in woodwork he would wait until I wasn't looking then accidentally on purpose step on my woodwork snapping it, so it was back to the drawing board, this happened all the time, and in metalwork, we had a furnace to heat the metal up so we could bend it and shape it into pokers, brushes companion sets etc, his little evil trick was to wait until I had finished whatever I was doing then shove it back in the furnace to burn beyond recognition, yes he was an evil bugger, I also remember having this enormous blind boil on the back of my neck, Gurr would creep up behind me and smack it with the flat side of a ruler, the pain was excruciating, and god knows why, but we turned out to be friends at school and a few years later we worked together as plasterers.

Although I was enjoying school, I realised I should have tried that bit harder instead of rushing my work, as I said I was quite good at certain subjects, these were the ones I would rush, nine times out of ten they were correct, but goodness me very untidy, which would always get me into trouble, I can recall our Form Teacher, explaining to us the GCE exams, we were shortly going to sit, he went round the classroom and one by one told that pupil his expectations of them, when he got to me, he said, Shortle you haven't got a hope in the world of passing in anything, whether on not that was a devious plan to give me a kick up the backside, or not, I do not know, but what it did do, was to push me to do something about it, I thought I'm buggerd if I'm going to let him say that, so I got my head down, and passed in ten subjects two of them with distinction, I remember going up on stage and collecting my pass certificates, my Teacher just said well done Shortle I knew you could do it.

To be quite honest, to me school was something you had to do, and not something I wanted to do, there were far too many other things to think about.

I was getting to the stage in life when I realised there was a difference between boys and girls, but I'm sure that I didn't really understand what, anyway a new family had moved in down the road, just before Pleasant View, where Barry Nash lived, it is a detached Kent weatherboard Chalet Bungalow, called Rosedene, the new Family were the Courtmans, they had move from Frythe Way, a Council Estate just on the edge of Cranbrook Town, apparently Mr Courtman was left the property when his Mum died, the only thing I can remember about Mr Courtmans Mum was, she was blind and kept geese, and heaven forbid if you went near them, then there was Mrs Courtman, quite a chubby Lady and someone I got to know very well, a bit later on in life, they had three girls, Brenda the oldest, Anne the middle one then Hazel the youngest, Brenda was just that little bit older than us lot, so we didn't have much to do with her, however Anne and Hazel we did get to know, and it wasn't too long before they started to pop up to Henniker to play with the Western Girls, at that time I was far too shy to speak to them, I would peak round the side of the window, I remember Anne used to wear these short tight hot pants, she was only about eleven, Mum would say, look at that girl she knows she is pretty, look at her teasing the boys, Mum knew I liked her and although I never managed to go out with her for several years, she used to say one day you will marry that girl, I told her not to be so silly.

I was Thirteen and I was looking to earn a bit more money, I decided to see if I could do another paper round, in addition to the one I already had, I heard through the grapevine that Newsagents Dykes were looking for someone to do an evening round, off I went to apply for the job, they were all aware of the fact I already had a morning round, I suppose they must have had a word with the other Newsagents, as they offered me the job there and then, I was also doing a morning job at Lees, plus a Sunday paper round with Dykes, David would help me with this one, I did these until I left School at the ripe old age of fifteen.

There were quite a few characters that lived in or around Hartley, for instance and old Lady we nicknamed Dolly Harris, don't ask me why she was called that, because I couldn't tell you, she had this old push bike, which would squeak like hell, we would tell her that the wheels were going round, Dolly would get off the bike have a look then get back on, and pedal away, she always wore an old light coloured Macintosh with a head scarf, I think she must have been a little backward, but kids don't pick up on that, to us it was someone we could tease, but at least it was kids being lippy and nothing else, we never ever caused anyone physical pain. Not like kids of today, then there was Rolly Parker, the Son of Mr Parker who owned the greengrocers at the top of the hill, Rolly was a bit backward as well, but able to deliver groceries for his Dad, on his trades bike, we thought he was the Boyfriend of Marge Leonard at No 6 Henniker Cotts, he seemed strange, but quite harmless, he had this strange habit of shrieking out the word Cuckoo at regular intervals I believe he was taken into care somewhere along the line as his parents couldn't cope with his ever increasing violent outbursts.

Johnny Boy was back to his usual mad ways, and this time he had teamed up with a bloke called, Johnny Ovenden, who had convinced Johnny Boy that he was a singer songwriter, and if they put there talents together, they would without doubt produce a top selling record, now I'm no expert on this sort of thing, but it was painfully obvious that they had as much chance at making this project happen as winning the pools, this went on for months, there they were, the two Johnnies one playing the piano ok-ish the other trying to sing which was absolutely awful, although they kept in touch, the novelty and enthusiasm of making it big time in the music industry was just a figment of their imaginations.

Another occupation he pursued, after his regular visits to the tip collecting electrical bits, and fiddling about in the loft with radios and televisions, was television repairs which we dreaded, because we were involved, televisions in those days were as big as fridges, small screens sitting inside dam great wooden boxes, Johnny Boys technique was to sit the TV on the table, remove the back then fiddle inside whilst the bloody thing was switched on, now so far it seems my involvement is nil, infact to me it was like Chinese torture, imagine Johnny Boy fiddling in the back of the TV, whilst I had to sit on a stool with a mirror facing Johnny Boy so he could see what was going on, I may have to sit there for what seemed like hours, and god help me if I moved or tipped the mirror, he was obviously very talented, but I believe absolutely crackers.

His urge to turn his ideas into reality was relentless, he came home one afternoon from the Hartley Duke and said he was given a fire surround because they were renovating the place, we had no idea what he was talking about, anyway, he had borrowed some old pick up truck which was outside, David and myself were summons outside, to help carry this contraption into the house, it wasn't a fire surround at all, but three pieces of wall cladding about eight feet high by four feet wide, they were in dark wood, with very heavy ornate carvings all over them, absolutely hideous, there was also a floor to ceiling mantle piece, all this was going to be installed in our very small council house, with our help, he managed to get them into the house, where it stayed just propped up against the walls for ages, then one day a couple of blokes came along and took it away. I suppose he must have sold it, All we had to do was to wait for the next contraption or idea to raise its ugly head.

It was getting near Christmas, I realise that I haven't mentioned anything about Christmas so far, I suppose although we always got excited in our own way, and knew it was never easy for Mum, our expectations were never too high, to help matters Mum tried to pay so much a week into a Christmas Club at Piper's the Grocers, in Cranbrook, they would deliver this big box of goodies every Christmas Eve, Mum would lock it up in the cupboard until Christmas morning, I'm not sure if it was to keep it away from us or Johnny Boy! I think Christmas Eve was more exciting than Christmas Day, us kids would all get together listening to the radio banging out carols whilst we made paper chains, Mum would be busy making sausage rolls and mince pies etc, and sipping one, two or more Sherries. Johnny Boy, nine times out of ten would be up the pub playing the piano for free drinks.

One Christmas Eve it was snowing a blizzard, we were out playing and supposedly clearing the snow from the paths and generally having a whale of a time, it was so much like Christmas should be, I remember the Street lights being on, and as the snow came down, it looked so magical as it passed the bright street light, I could have stayed out in the snow all night, in the distance was a Lady walking through the snow, as she got ever nearer I could tell it was the Lady that lived in the posh house a bit further down the road, between the bus stop and Mr Parkers shop. I don't know why but I decided to sweep a path for her, all the way to her house, she was so thankful, she gave me a little money and said she will always remember me as the Boy that swept a path in the snow for her, thinking I could perhaps make a few bob doing this, I decided to try the same thing on the next passerby, unfortunately, nobody else came along, anyway it was well past our time to go indoors, go to bed and wait for Christmas Day. Because we were four Boys, and Eileen, us Boys had to sleep in one bedroom, in a double bed, we would top and tail, IE David and me at the top, Christ and Peter at the bottom, most nights before we settled down and went to sleep, it was story time, I was the one that told the best tales, so it was always me, they were mainly about a family that live on Causton Road council estate, just off Cranbrook High Street, they were the Macey's, plus a woman called Marge

Cogger, she used to trot about like Barbara Winsor, she had all the assets, but unfortunately not the looks, I got the stories listening to Mum having chats with different people, I would earwig to get more information to help with my next rendition, I must have been quite good at storytelling, because I had to come up with something most nights, god knows what drivel I said, but we were always in hysterics, I would also try to give each character some strange sort of accent, and believe me, by the end of each story I had almost lost my voice. It was good harmless fun, and by the time they would eventually allow me to stop, we would all go out like lights.

On Christmas morning like most kids we were up at the crack of dawn, creep downstairs to see what delights there were, we always had the compulsory stocking, usually Mums Nylons, which were stuffed mainly with oranges and nuts, and perhaps a cracker, although we never got much, Mum always did her best to give us a lovely Christmas, I remember one year, in the corner of the front room was this big thing wrapped up, it was for all us Boys, it didn't take us long to rip the wrapping off, to find it was a fortress, complete with draw bridge, it was fantastic, Johnny Boy had made it out of thin ply, it looked a proper job, even the walls seemed real, they were all rough, just like stone, he had put glue all over it then dusted it with sand, and finished it off with paint, he even made some soldiers, and bits and pieces, it was great.

We never went short of anything really, as they say, as long as your belly is full, you have a roof over your head and cloths on your back, then what is there to worry about.

It was New Years Eve and Mum had made arrangements to go out with Jimmy Miller, to see the New Year in, on the odd occasion when Mum did manage to get out, she would ask a Lady by the name of Pat Baker to child mind, we liked her, she was good fun, and really easy going, on this particular evening she arrived all dressed up, which was strange, anyway after Mum was gone, she explained that she also had arranged to go out, she asked us if we would be prepared to look after ourselves, she even offered to give us the money Mum had given her, Pat said she would be back before Mum, so nobody would be any the wiser, she was waving a ten bob note, our eyes lit up, to us it was a bloody fortune, so of course we said we would, Pat left, but unfortunately it all went pear shaped, because she never came back, needless to say, when Mum found out she went berserk, took the ten bob note back, so our dreams of having all this dosh went out of the window, I think after that little episode Mum felt we could look after ourselves, so that's how it was left, we were sworn to secrecy and told never to tell Johnny Boy, we never said a word because we were all terrified of him, and hated his smash ups, which still happened on a regular basis, the house had all sorts of tea stains, chip marks etc as a reminder of his tempers, the only time we would see him happy go lucky, was when he brought one of his friends home, he was the perfect gentleman, but as soon as his friend or friends left, he could quite easily, for absolutely no reason at all snap, and start to throw things about.

At school I began to get to know other Boys, one in particular was a John Dean, or Deno as we got to call him, I believe they moved to Cranbrook from London, his parents took over the Pub called the Duke, that was situated at the top end of the high street, his Mum was a small Lady we would call Mummer Moose, and his Dad, a big well rounded Man, we would call Jimace old Bean, only because Deno called them that, Jimace had hardly any hair, and what he did have, he would flatten down with cooking lard, he would go into the wash room at the back of the Pub always with just a vest on, give himself a quick slues, wet and dry his hair which took no time at all, he spent more time flattening his hair down with lard than anything else, he wasn't a healthy Man, he was always taking short intakes of air, as if he was struggling to breath, Deno was the only child, spoilt rotten, he could have almost anything he wanted, he had this fascination for guns, at thirteen he owned several .177's and .22 air rifles, plus a couple of air pistols, which were easy to buy if you had the money, the cheapest was the air pistol that required loading with air by pushing the end part of the barrel back into the outer barrel which would load the gun, then place a pellet into the back of the pistol making it ready to fire, I managed to get one of those, but it was pretty useless, as you fire it, you could see the slug come out, it had no range or power at all, however if you could afford the under lever type, which Deno did, this had a fixed barrel, but a lever under the barrel that loaded it up, with much more air pressure, the slugs in those would fly, he also had powerful air rifles, the .22's were by far the most powerful, he also owned an old 303, he was always telling me that he could kill a rabbit as far away as Sissinghurst, which was two miles down the road, I used to say, that's all well and good if you could see the bloody thing.

Deno's parents owned a small holding, just up the road, we would spend hours at that place, they kept rabbits chickens, ducks and geese, we would take our air rifles with us, and have air rifle fights, we would hide in sheds then fire slugs at each other, how dangerous was that, with more luck than judgement we never hit each other.

One day a seagull flew over, and we actually shot it down, when it crashed to the ground we couldn't believe how big it was. We were shitting ourselves thinking we would get into loads of trouble if anyone found out, so we decided to bury it in Jimace's small holding.

One day, we decided to go to Angley Woods with our guns, the woods were situated next to the road that went passed Enfield's Farm, it was, and still is a very big wood, and part Forest, it must cover hundreds of acres, we had been there many times, there was so much to do, we could keep ourselves occupied for hours, we used to do something we would call cattle bending, haven't got a clue where that name came from, but basically what it was, look for a young Silver Birch that was nice and straight, but most importantly bendy, the object of the exercise was to climb to almost the top, grab hold of the main trunk with both hands, then throw ourselves outwards, bringing the top of the tree with us, if we chose well, we would gently float to the ground whilst hanging onto the tree, we were very good at choosing the right Silver Birch as I don't ever remember braking a tree.

Now and then our gang, would have a fight with the Frythe Home Guard, who's leader was Gary Blanch, Lunchy the hop picking tractor driver's, younger Brother', it never came to much, and it was all about taking control of an area in Angley Wood, we called the clearing, it was surrounded by Beach trees, I can't remember too much about it, but the Frythe Home Guard always won.

One day when we were walking through the woods, Deno shot me up the arse with his airgun, it went through my coat and trousers, it had to be dug out, did that hurt, Deno thought it was funny, at the time we were looking to find somewhere out of the way, deep into the woods to have some target practice, bottles would be placed, then knocked over if we hit them, of course Deno always did the best, because he had the better gun. Deno would shoot at anything and everything, even his mums washing, he was a sod.

I loved going to Deno's especially on a Sunday afternoon, the Pub would be shut, Deno would be allowed to mess around in the bars, it was great fun, but as always, being with Deno, always had an element of danger, even a simple thing like playing darts, you had to be on your toes he couldn't be trusted, his dart would go into anything but the dart board, his Mum would moan but Deno didn't seem to care, Jimace Old Bean would be upstairs having a nap. I never ever heard Deno get a proper rollicking from either of them.

One Sunday afternoon I had my first taste of Alcohol, I will never forgot, it was barley wine, I was not quite fourteen, there I was being tanked up by Deno with barley wine, I'm sure it didn't take much to get me drunk, I was so drunk, I remember Deno laughing, he kicked me out of the side door where all the barrels were, and locked it, I was on my own, my way to make my way to Henniker, god knows how I made it home, my last recall of that day was, David, Chris and Peter finding me, after that it was a blur, I'm sure I was ill for quite a while, I don't believe I touched another drop until I left school.

These sorts of antics with Deno continued until we left school, Deno got a job with the forestry commission with Ron Day, or (Honey Bunny as we called him) and I think a guy named David Dowsing, however we did keep in touch, more of this later.

Back home things carried on much the same, Mum still working her socks off, Johnny Boy still being a pain in the arse, I remember him coming back from somewhere or another, but this time not on his own, he had the audacity to bring a woman home, I can't remember to much, but I do know, she stayed for a while, and gathered it was his girlfriend, Mum was livid, I remember her saying to him, how dare you bring another Woman to stay in this house, but I recon Mum was quite happy about it, as she could now do as she pleased, this without doubt was the beginning of the end of any relationship they may have had, unfortunately it was to drag on for a few more years yet, poor Mum.

If I remember correctly, when this Woman left, Johnny Boy went with her, we were all hoping that was the last of him, but before too long he ended up back on the doorstep, probably smooth talked Mum to let him in, to think about it, things for a short while were quite civilised, but that soon changed.

One afternoon whilst Johnny Boy was away, I remember Mum not feeling very well, she said she was going to bed, before too long Mum called out for me to come upstairs, as I entered her bedroom she told me not to look under the bed, if she had said nothing, I wouldn't have looked, but of course I did, I noticed something wrapped up in newspaper and quite a bit of blood, she gave me this note, and strict instructions, to run over to the Old people's home where she worked, to go through the main arched entrance, and make sure I gave this note to one of the nurses, my heart was pumping, I knew something was wrong, but didn't know what, I found a nurse, she read the note, told me to stay where I was, I think she must have called the Doctor, the nurse took me home, told us all to play in the garden, whilst she went upstairs to see Mum, the Doctor arrived, and after a while, everything calmed down, I learnt later Mum had a miscarriage.

It was a frightening experience and I'm sure just as much so for Mum, but thankfully Mum soon got back to her old self.

I was now fourteen, with one more year left at school, I had no idea what this meant, except, I would be able to find myself a job, until then, I continued doing my paper rounds and Saturday morning job.

So I just continued doing what kids do, one day we were on our way home from Henniker Pond, where we had been Pike fishing, the trick was to first of all fish for small roach, which is illegal now, and use them as live bait, bloody cruel I know, but that's how it was done in those days, we were very good at catching Pike, they are evil looking things with rows of sharp teeth, it wasn't very often we went away without catching at least one, it was fantastic struggling with the rod, and line trying to land them, but very rewarding when we did, I'm sure we actually ate one or two of them, we loved to fish, there were a couple of other ponds around, one the Haunted down Swattenden lane, I caught a whacking great Roach there on a daisy once, there was another pond, up a rough track near the Railway station, which was a good place to catch Tench, we found, the best time to catch Tench was at dusk. on our way home from Henniker Pond, after a day's fishing, we would play in a tree, that was growing out of the side of the ditch made by the doodle bug, it was right on the edge of Henniker Wood, we would often play around in this tree, as I was larking about, I sensed I was about to fall, as I fell my arm was behind my back with my elbow sticking out, and I do not know why I said it, but I shouted I'm going to break my arm, which I actually did, I remember my forearm had snapped, it looked just like a swans neck, I think David assisted whilst the others legged it home to tell Mum, I was in plaster for a few weeks, but at that age something like that doesn't seem a problem.

Most of us injured ourselves one way or another, David had a couple, first one was when he was about eight, he was on his way to Cubs, and Boys being Boys he decided to swerve past a Post Office Van, that was either coming out or going into the Post office yard, anyway David swerved past the front of the van, hitting it, ending up on the ground with his bike under the van, he had what he thought to be just a stiff neck, unfortunately a couple of weeks later he was taken to hospital, as he was in such pain, and had this big lump sticking out of the back of his neck, they soon discovered that the collision had been severe enough to dislodge one of the vertebra in his neck, they put the poor bugger in traction with weights that would hopefully get him mended, it seemed to do the trick, but unfortunately in his late teens he developed spodalities, sadly David has had to live with the worsening problem since that feted day, and to be honest, he has the heart of a Lion, not once has he ever felt sorry for himself, he has a fantastic outlook on life, he will tell you how it is, no pussy footing around, like it or lump it, that's David, he also had another accident on his AJS motorbike, going through the series of bends at Tubslake, I understand he was showing off to some girls, taking his hands off the bike, sadly a milk lorry was coming the other way, David's shoulder and arm took a right old bashing, as the lorry drove past, somehow he managed to stay on the bike, as the lorry disappeared he managed to just about stop his bike by a bus stop that had people waiting, he was a right old mess, he asked them to get an ambulance, he was admitted with a broken shoulder and horrible cuts and bruises, I picked him up a day or two later in my Hillman

Minx. Chris had a bad one as well, he was walking home from school, with I think either his jacket or satchel slung over his shoulder, as a lorry passed it caught one of those, pulling him into the lorry, then lucky for him knocked him back onto the pavement, he suffered a fractured skull, and was in a bad way for quite a while, now we just laugh and say, that's what has made him so intelligent, a week or so before then, I was supposed to be going to Sunday school. I had Eileen on the crossbar, and instead of going towards Cranbrook, to the Catholic Church. I decided at the last minute to turn left down Angley Road, with intentions of going to Angley Woods, at that time the road had a bit of a hill, it had just been re gritted, as we got halfway down the hill, Eileen got her foot lodged between the front forks and the top of the wheel, she was launched off the bike into the bank, whilst I was thrown over the handle bars, ending up going down the road on my face, Eileen was fine, but I was a right mess, I had to have some sort of poultice on my face, to get the grit out, it was bloody painful, trying to explain that one to Mum, was impossible, so I had to tell the truth oh dear.

It was just a day or two before I was back on my bike, amazingly it wasn't badly damaged, more scratches than anything else, I must admit I was a bit of a show off so the odd tumble was always going to be part of my biking experiences, quite often I would try to beat the bus from Henniker to Cranbrook, and nine times out of ten I would do just that, one day the bus conductor got so annoyed with my escapades, he collared me and gave me a right telling off, mind you it never stopped me, I was having fun. It's just a shame, there was no proper organised bike tracks to keep us out of trouble like there is today, mind you we seemed to do ok, finding things to do, was just part of the day, as kids, we could leave home at nine am and most times not return till tea time, we would go on all sorts of expeditions, normally it would be myself, David, Barry Nash, Chris, Peter and Bobby Western, not only to Angley Woods, but also to Robin's Wood and Bedgebury Forest.

Both of these were situated just off the Hawhurst road, Robin's wood was first up, a little way passed the Railway Tavern, turn left immediately before the Hartley Stores down a rough unmade track, we would follow this track all the way to the end, to be greeted by a five bar gate which was to stop the cattle getting out of the farm, this land is owned by the Bridges, the farm was known as Bridger's Farm.

The other side of the gate was a field that climbed quite dramatically to the right, this lead to Robins Wood, in the Spring the field was always full of wild flowers, it really must have been a lovely place, but to us Kids, just a short cut to Robins Wood, at the top of the field just before the wood, the view was amazing, I can't remember too much about it, but I have been told how beautiful it was, I wonder if it is like that today? Perhaps I will go back and have a look for myself one day. Robins wood was also just as magical, it was quite a small wood, with a stream that ran right through the middle, the stream was set in a valley, and I can still recall how clear the water was, the stream meandered all the way down to an overgrown pond almost opposite the road that went to Bedgebury Forest, the pond was known as Tubslake, the story goes, this was where the Smugglers hid tubs of spirit. Robin's Wood was never over used, we seldom saw anyone else there, again in the Spring it was a blanket of Bluebells, daffodils, Primroses, and all sorts of wild flowers, we would set up camp, always have our Billy Can, light a fire, bring the Billy Can to the boil with water from the stream, not forgetting the piece of wood, for a cup of smoke free tea, make a few sandwiches, and be quite happy with our lot.

Then there was Bedgebury Forest, a bit further on, after the Hartley Duke we had to climb quite a steep hill, go over the crest, then drop back down again, past Tubs Lake on our left, then almost immediately turn right into an unmade road, which eventually got us to Bedgbury, it was a fair old trek, but we could at least use our bikes on this expedition, probably from Henniker it was about three miles, Bedgebury was completely different to Robin's Wood, it was owned by the Forestry Commission, and even then it was a very popular place for the public to visit, there was this fantastic Lake deep in the Forest, it was enormous, and was surrounded by very tall pine and fir trees, with a host of other trees mingled in, it was awash everywhere with rhododendrons of all colours they were absolutely gorgeous, a lot of the trees had information boards, telling you their name, type, what part of the world they originated from, the one we always found fascinating was a massive great tree that was so soft, you could punch it without hurting yourself, can't remember it's name. As we walked, we didn't ride our bikes, not allowed, it was like being midgets in a land of massive trees, the roots were poking out of the ground everywhere, whilst the trees towered above, letting the light filter through where it could.

We had to be on our best behaviour, but it never spoilt our fun, always took our fishing rods in case we felt like a bit of fishing, there is also a posh school on the outskirts of the Forest, I'm sure it's called Bedgebury School. The worst thing about this expedition was the journey home, it was up hill most of the way, we were all tired, so it took us forever to get home, we were always late when we went to Bedgebury, no mobile phones in those days for our Mums to find out where we were, eventually we arrived, back home safe but tired, funny how Mums know, she just said, you've been to Bedgebury haven't you. I think we were all little buggers, but nice little buggers.

Around this time there was excitement for us in Henniker Woods, one morning we could see from the bottom of our garden a tractor and trailer making its way down to the wood, the entry to the wood was through a farm gate by the road, next to Leonards, it allowed the Farmer access to his field, we thought it was the Farmer, but being nosey we decided to go down there, and have a look, we were cautious when we arrived, so we just watched from a safe distance, after a while, one of the Men said hello, asked where did we come from. We told them we lived in Henniker Cottages, up the top of the field, and that we wanted to have a look, they informed us they were there to thin the wood out, apparently something they do every so many years, as it allows the trees more room to grow again, and at the same time, they can make use of the trees they had felled, they explained that some of the timber would be used to make pit props, so the Miners can prop up the tunnels as they dig their way through the mine, mining was still a major part of Britain then, also they would use some of the smaller timber to make fencing, they told us to leave it for a day or two then come back, there will be more to see, for a couple of days we could hear the faint sound of their chain saws which seemed to be going nonstop, there was also smoke coming out through the trees, we couldn't wait to go back, on the second day we went back, goodness me Henniker woods certainly started to look different, they had cut through quite a lot of the wood already, there was a self made work area in case of rain, they had constructed it out of timber lashed together, with a huge tarpaulin over the top, it looked great, I thought it made our attempts of making a camp look quite feeble, they knocked timbers into the ground, then crossed them about waist high, this allowed the timbers to lay in the crossed section and stay firm whilst being cut and worked on, we were mesmerised with what they were doing, the speed they shaved the timer, the way they were splitting the wood to make the fence panels, then weaving it in out of poles to complete the finished panel. When they packed up for the day we would nip down there, to poke the fire and play around on the stacks of pit props, they were there for a quite a while, and we missed them when they were gone.

The wood was now so clear and tidy, we could go to places in that wood that were unreachable, we even found that next to the pond where we used to fish, was another smaller pond, they had left the odd length of timber so we decided to attempt to make a raft, we made a platform by tying it together, then scouted around for some water drums which we used to keep the thing afloat, after quite a few attempts it actually worked, until the string/rope started to come undone and the raft parted company with each other, luckily we were not too far out, so all was ok, I think after that we got fed up with being on the open seas, so it was time to move on.

It wasn't too long before I left school, I still didn't have a job, but in those days it was taken for granted, that everyone would find employment of some sort or another, school leavers were still being encouraged to join the Forces, something I wasn't interested in, so I was hoping to find a job locally, I still had my paper rounds and Saturday morning job, Mum advised me to stick with them until I found fulltime employment.

Chapter 4.
Leaving School. Welcome to the real World.

The day had arrived, and all of a sudden, it was different, no more School, no more long summer holidays, oh no, I had to start looking for a job, fortunately, I know it wasn't many days before Mrs Nash (Barries Mum) came up to see my Mum, she explained her Father Horace Burgess, that owned one of the Butchers shops in Cranbrook, was looking for a butchers Boy, she had put my name forward, Barry! Mr Burgess Grandson, was a year or two younger than me, so he wasn't available even if he wanted the job, I was so excited, Mrs Nash told me to go and see him on the Wednesday afternoon, shops always closed half day on a Wednesday, Mum made sure I was respectable, gave me a few words of advice, including being polite.

Wednesday arrived, I was so nervous, this was all new to me, and the chance of a fulltime job within a week of leaving school wow, I hadn't a clue what to say, didn't know what was a decent wage for a school leaver, all I did know, was I was a hard worker, and someone keen to learn, I remember getting there far too early, so I decided to just bike around anywhere to waste time, I knew the importance of being punctual, but didn't want to look too keen, the time had arrived, I was that nervous, I had to push myself to knock on his door. Mrs Burgess came to the door, I told her who I was, and she told me to come in, she introduced me to Mr Burgess, he was a short Man with big ears, very stern looking, which made me even more nervous, he sat me down, asked me a few questions, including laying out the ground rules, by this stage it was a mixture of emotions for me, half of me was shitting bricks, the other half was a tremendous feeling of excitement and achievement, after a chat he took me downstairs to the shop, I remember him being very thorough, most of it I didn't take in, but what I did get out of the conversation was, my initial job description, which included, delivering meat on a trades bike, something I could easily do, because of my paper round experience, and on a Saturday go in the Van and help deliver further afield, also to help out in the cutting room, and learn as much as I could.

I was nodding and hopefully smiling in the right places, by this time I definitely wanted the job, I was on tender hooks, thinking please put me out of my misery, he asked me a few more questions, told me the pay was one pound fifty shilling a week, which I thought fantastic, but really it was sod all, he asked me if I would like the job, I said yes, he then said ok Boy, start next Tuesday eight o clock, don't be late. So there I was just two weeks after my fifteenth birthday with a job.

I knew Mum would be at home chewing her finger ends, I couldn't get home quick enough to tell her, I've never biked up that hill out of Cranbrook so fast. Mum knew I got the job before I said a word, I think it was the way I jumped off my bike whilst it was still travelling down the front garden, I got a glimpse of Mum through the front window, I think for her! It was just as important as it was for me, I was at the point of crying, I think I held myself together, but Mum couldn't hold back her feelings, bless her.

Mum told me to go and tell Mrs Nash, I got the job, thank her for putting a good word in, Mrs Nash was so pleased. It seemed like eternity, waiting for Tuesday, but in the meantime, I think I was in a daze, to me I had achieved the most important thing of my young life.

My next task was to tell the paper shops, that I had got myself a fulltime job and wouldn't be able to work for them after Sunday, they were a bit put out, but wished me all the best, and both said I had been a good paper Boy. My house was in order, I was ready, or thought I was for the big wide world.

Tuesday arrived, I was early, but not as early as everyone else, I parked my bike round the back and made my way into the shop, Mr Burgess introduced me to the other chap that worked there, his name was Bob Nicholls, he had worked for Horace for many years, he was a very short Man, almost as round as he was tall, he also had this enormous bulge in his trousers that seemed to swing about as he walked, I was told somewhere along the line it was a double rupture, and he was too frightened to have something done about it, Bob's main job, was in the cutting room out the back, preparing the meat ready for sale, and delivery, which also included making the sausages, trussing the chickens, etc. He would help and serve in the shop, if things got too busy for Mr Burgess, and also do the odd delivery in the van if a customer needed something in a hurry, Mrs Burgess took the money, she had this pay booth customer side of the shop, it was a bit like a Punch and Judy box, with a serving hatch. I was fitted out with a brown coat, far too big for me, a blue and white stripped apron, Bob showed me how to fold it over when I was delivering, so it looked clean, couldn't understand that, why not just take it off? once kitted out I was shown the delivery procedure, how to take the money from the customer, not to leave meat unattended in the trades bike's basket, as it could walk or dogs etc may get hungry, it wasn't long before the orders were ready, and my first delivery was under way, it was quite a big round, I had to return to the shop on several occasions, to collect more orders, if I remember my first outing was, up the high street, which was a long gentle hill all the way to the memorial, which I found hard going when the basket was full of orders, stopping now and again to deliver, including an estate just before the Memorial on the left, known as Goddard's Close, they were Airy Houses, which meant they are built out of concrete slabs, looked a bit posh in those days, I would deliver to one of the Goddard's Green Cottages, next to the field, Mum and I used to visit when they were cutting the hay, then it was down Angley Road past Enfield's

Farm, delivering all the way, if I had deliveries on board I would go all the way to Willesley Pound, then turn right back onto the Cranbrook Road, doing the odd delivery to Courts Style on your right, where the Fosters went after Orchard Way, then down a steep hill toward Cranbrook, into Waterloo Road, which is where the Grammar school was, I liked Waterloo Road with all its beamed houses. Then it was up Stone Street into the High Street, Burgess the Butchers was just round the corner.

Into the shop for another basket full of deliveries, then back down the Stone Street, turning right just before Waterloo Road, which would take me up Windmill Hill Road, as you turned right, there is a fantastic view of the windmill, which in those days was still a working mill, I would do the odd delivery up the hill, usually into the Old house at Home, which was a Pub but sadly a private dwelling even then, about two hundred yards further on, take a right turn, into Frythe Way, the biggest council estate in Cranbrook, quite a few deliveries here, once that was done, then off down Golford Road, now and again I would deliver here and there including to the Old Cloth Hall, which is up a lane just before the cemetery it's a very historic house, a few more deliveries, then back to the shop, most days I was delivering up to lunchtime.

Mr Burgess seemed pleased with me and I was soon feeling at home, I think my next job was cleaning, such as the sausage machine, I remember being shown how to clean the cutting block, it was done using a wooden block that had steel brushes, first you wiped all the excess meat and fat off, then dusted the block with sawdust followed by an awful lot of scrubbing with the steel brush, it was hard work but very rewarding when it was clean, every block had to be done like this, each night before we shut, there were a further two in the shop, I was keen to learn, and knew it would be time before that let me loose with a sharp knife and chopper, on the meat itself, my first day was drawing to a close, the worst job was always cleaning out the mincer, one that I was lumbered with all the time, the window display trays had to be taken out, all washed, then once the window was cleaned, the trays went back, with a displays to make it look presentable overnight, I soon found out that working for a living, wasn't as easy as one thought, but I enjoyed it and wasn't afraid of hard work. I was about to leave when Mr Burgess called me to one side and told me that he was very pleased with my first day, gave me a pound of sausages, and said see you in the morning, I was bloody knackered, but so happy, I felt great, Mum was pleased with the sausages, although initially she thought I may have nicked them.

I got home, and after dinner I was ready for my bed, I then realised that many of the things I used to do, would not happen anymore. By then anyway David, Chris, Peter and Eileen were doing their own things.

Morning soon came around, but I was bright as a button, and couldn't wait to get to work, I was aware of how my day would pan out, although hoping, this maybe the day I get to do something different, every morning before the shop opened the floors had to be dusted with sawdust, I loved doing this job, so much so, that I hated anyone walking on it, as to me there was nothing better than seeing a butchers floor dusted evenly with sawdust, strange thing to like, but there you go, as the weeks came and went, I was beginning to be shown bits and pieces, my first job was to cut up and prepare the meat for the sausages, in those days, when you cook them, sausages would explode, simply because, a very high percentage of the mix was fat, this all went into the mincer, then into a large steel bin, which already had a measure of bread crumbs and seasoning. I then mixed it up thoroughly by hand, I recon 75% of this mix was fat, breadcrumbs and seasoning, with no more that 25% meat, you would never get away with it today, but funny enough, everyone that bought our sausages loved them, the sausage making machine in those days, wasn't electric, oh no, it was done by hand, it was a very simple piece of kit, basically there was a metal drum about two feet long, which was fixed to a strong metal bench, to one end of the drum, you screwed a tapered pipe, this was where the mix came out, the other end was open, and was the full diameter of the drum, this is where the mix goes in, once the drum is full of sausage meat, the open end is then closed, the closed cap has a plunger fixed to it, there is a handle on the outside, which as you wind, it pushes the plunger towards the front of the barrel, in turn forcing the meat out through the tapered pipe, ready to be made into sausages, now this is where the knack is, whilst turning the handle, and as the mix comes out of the tube you have to feed the sausage meat into the skins, with the other hand, this takes quite a lot of practice, to get right, they have to be of equal size and always be eight to the pound.

I must admit it took me quite a while to get the hang of it, but as they say practice makes perfect, but the problem was, I couldn't afford to keep making mistakes, as I Horace hates waste.

Within six months I was fairly competent at cutting up most types of meat, I could cut up a hind or fore quarter of beef, chop a pig or lamb in half which was quite a knack boning and rolling joints was easy enough, but Horace would always a keep watchful eye, as he hated meat being left on the bone, because it was wasteful.

I was now part of the furniture, so I began to gain confidence and show my personality, at times I got a bit too cheeky, and started to get up to all sorts of capers, poor Bob was my main target, in the cutting room were two very large freezers, constantly being used, as the door was shut, the freezer light would go out and the fan would come on, one day as Bob went into the freezer I shut the door, and dropped a skewer into a couple of holes in the door, which stopped it from coming open and made it impossible for him to get out, I left him in there for a short while, but long enough for him to get bloody cold, and bloody furious, which he was on both accounts, I expected him to tell Horace but he never said a word, so out of respect I never did anything like that again, when Horace was in a good mood I would get away with murder, so if I wanted to be a bit silly I had to get my timing right, one day I was working on an Ox head, which entailed, taking the cheeks off. Sawing it in half, and taking the brains out, quite disgusting for a fifteen year old, now this is the silly bit, I decided to remove the eyes so I could hang them out of my top pocket, once in my pocket I walked into the shop, just to see how long it would take for anyone to notice, believe me it didn't take long at all, good job Horace was in a good mood, when he noticed he just smirked and told me to go out the back and get rid of them, another bit of stupidity of mine, as I was trussing chicken's, out the back, on the cutting block, that sat in a recess, the recess had a sash window, which we opened in the warm weather, when I removed the chickens head, I would lean out of the window and throw the head skywards, the object of the exercise was to try and get it to land in the guttering above, the car park of the George Hotel was opposite, so now and again, I would pop over there to see how many were hanging out of the gutter, if it came back down, I would rush outside and retrieve it, God knows how many heads had stayed up there, this silly game continued for some time. Until one day, Horace came and had a word with me, he had just got back from lunch, only to inform me that he was sitting having his lunch in the bay window above the cutting room, when all a sudden he saw these bloody chickens heads flying past his window, little did I know his dining table upstairs was right next to his window, he went bloody ape shit, and made me get a ladder to clear the lot out, there were loads of them all hanging over the guttering, yes I got away with murder.

Mr Burgess's Butcher Shop, it's the beamed building, now Lloyds Pharmacy.

I always looked forward to Saturdays, going out in the van to help the Lady that was in charge of the deliveries, if I remember her name was Pat Smith, she was probably around forty, I thought she was lovely. She had enormous breasts, which were accentuated with the money bag strap that would go over her shoulder then lie diagonally between those big boobies, then re-join the bag that rested on her opposite hip, when she couldn't make it her husband would stand in, he was a nice enough bloke, the only thing I could remember about him, was the awful aftershave he would wear, it was so strong and sweet you could almost taste it, ugh, I much preferred to ogle at his wife.

The van was a little grey Austin A35, it wasn't too long before I started to fiddle with the gear leaver, trying to change gear, Pat would sometimes let me change gear whilst she was driving, and when we were down a private road she would let me steer, to be honest this was the main reason I enjoyed Saturday's so much, and sometimes if we parked on a hill, and I was left in the van, I would get into the drivers seat, knock it out of gear, release the hand brake, then steer it down the hill, Pat would go bonkers.

As I got more and more confident, I would start the van up, experiment with the pedals, Pat had explained what each pedal was for, I would start it up and begin to drive it, maybe only a few feet, mainly so Pat didn't notice it had been moved, I was getting more and more confident, and when we were in Hartley, there was a private road called Mead Road, right at the end, the road would go all the way round just like a roundabout with the odd house around it's perimeter, Pat was soon confident enough to let me drive the van at Mead Road, which was great, something I looked forward to every week, fabulous fun for a fifteen year old.

I'm sure Pat was getting concerned about my driving excursions, it was getting to the stage where she always wondered each time she walked out of the customers front gate, where the van would be, it most certainly wasn't outside the house, because I was yet to be able to reverse, one day I decided to try and select reverse, which I found difficult, I asked Pat but she wouldn't show me, as on no account did she want me to drive the butchers van backwards, I could hardly drive it forwards.

But the inevitable would happen, I wanted to be able to engage reverse, eventually I discovered how it was done, mystery over, so now I could drive backwards and forwards, obviously I did not mention to Pat that I had found reverse, no I decided to keep it under my hat, I was having a whale of a time, driving backwards, forwards, backwards, forwards, etc, until one morning I decided to try and reverse all the way around this circular road, all was fine until I began to get nearer and nearer the inside of the road, where it would drop away quite steeply, with one of those metal railing fences, right in the dip, yes you've guessed it I was reversing, and dropped the rear wheel over the edge, panic stations, I tried and tried to get the van free, without any success Pat seemed to be gone for hours, by the time she appeared, there was smoke coming from the engine compartment, along with a horrible burning smell. I had burnt the clutch out, as well as scratched the van to buggery all down one side, Pat I think was in shock, I was expecting a major rollicking, but she said nothing, I think she must have called the shop, and explained the situation, as it wasn't late long before Bob Nicholls arrived, he had some rope to pull the van out, then towed us back to the butchers, I was shitting myself, expecting instant dismissal, I didn't know what to say or do, in fact Mr Burgess seemed to carry on as if nothing had happened, I can tell you it was a long day, all sorts of things were going on in my head, and it wasn't until we had cleaned up and shut shop, that Horace, pulled me to one side, as he did, but I knew dam well it wasn't to thank me for a job well done, he just said Son have you got anything to tell me, I said yes and then went on to try and explain what I had done. I was expecting the worse, but still I got away with it, talk about a cat with nine lives, by my return on Tuesday morning it was as if nothing had happened, I think Bob Nicholls got a bit pissed off , there was I getting away with it all the time, and him, getting moaned at left right and centre, for no reason at all, he had every right to be miserable, with me being there under a year and him being a good honest employer for God knows how many years, taking all the flack, poor sod.

I decided it was time to try and grow up a bit; after all I was fast approaching my sixteenth birthday, I felt that both my quality and enthusiasm of work was not a problem, I just had to try and stop being so daft and stupid, something that is quite difficult for me not to do, as to some degree I am still very much like that to this very day, I suppose I have found a way to harness the stupidity, but I still try to be a bit of a laugh, you will see as you continue reading the book, I am always the joker in the pack, my wife recons it's because I'm an attention seeker, she is probably quite right.

On Monday's the shop was closed all day, Mr Burgess would trot off in his car to Hastings, to visit his brother, who lived just outside the Town, I think it was called Silvertown, he too owned a butchers shop, but also had his own slaughter house.

On the odd occasion he would invite me to come along, I remember the first time I was shown the slaughter house, it was awful, at the time there were a few pigs waiting to be killed, although it was quick, I think they knew, as the squealing was horrible, I hated it, once killed they were then hung up by the back legs, their throats were slit, apparently, they needed to drain the blood straight away, so the pork stays a very light colour, once drained they would slit the pig open from the throat to the belly, all the insides would fall out, blood and guts everywhere, then the offal was sorted, IE; heart, liver, kidneys, and tripe, which was the lining of the belly, it was quite a popular thing in those days, I think it was steamed, tripe and onions comes to mind. I never looked forward to my trips to Silvertown after that, but felt I should, to keep in his good books. Sometimes his Grandson Barry would come along for the ride, which made it just that little bit easier.

Mr Burgess was a great Bowles player, and I do believe he was the Captain of the Cranbrook Bowles Team, the Bowles Club was right opposite Cranbrook Primary School, when I was there I could remember all these old Men and Women arriving in their whites, Ladies in white pleated skirts, with white blouses and cardigans, finished off with white plimsolls, the men, white shirt, with a white or dark blue jacket with their Club badge on, white trousers and white plimsolls, hats must be worn, but it looked as if the choice of hat type was theirs, as long as it was white, Horace had a white cheese cutter, playing Bowels was a big part of Horace's life, his Brother played too, he very often had a day off to go and play somewhere or another, I do know he played until he was well into his eighties.

Mr Burgess's shop wasn't the only butchers shop in Cranbrook, there were two others, both in the Stone Street, Ratcliffe's were first up, they were on the left just after you turned into Stone Street, Wilks were a little bit further down on the right, just before Lees the Newsagents, so with three Butchers in the Town, competition was high, but they were all friendly with each other, and they thought nothing of helping each other out.

I remember one day I had just finished a delivery up the Frythe, I was on my way back to the shop, when it started raining cats and dogs, it was so bad I couldn't see a thing, but kept going, I had my head down to try and keep out of the rain, when all of a sudden in Stone Street right outside Wilkes's, I came to a sudden almighty stop, because I wasn't looking where I was going I went straight into the back of a lorry that was delivering meat to Wilkes's, my basket on the front of my bike flew across the road, I ended up sprawled on the road up against the back of the lorry, I think the meat company was Weddle's and I believe they are still in business to this day. Mr Wilks came rushing out of his shop to see if I was ok, he took me indoors and dried me off, took the micky out of me, then sent me on my way, as I said very helpful and friendly.

Now I had a wage, I was able to buy things, like clothes, the "in" thing was a Beetle Jacket, just like the Beetles wore, mine was brown corduroy very smart, the other piece of, "in" clothing, was the white Macintosh, this was all down to the series on television called the Man in a suitcase, he was always on the move, and nine times out of ten had this white Mac on, if you had one of those you were the business. In those days there were two types of fashion, you were either a Mod, or Rocker. A Mod was someone that drove a Scooter, had a beetle type haircut, and looked fairly smart, there means of transport would have been either a Vespa or Lambretta, I think the TV 175 was the one to have, this craze seemed to start when I was fifteen, so I had a bit of waiting to do before I could even think about owning my own scooter, let alone affording one, the Bloke at the time that owned the best Scooter was a chap by the name of Colin Bottle, and yes it was a TV. 175. Colin and his hangers on would congregate up the high street, outside his Dad's shop, I can't remember what type of shop it was, but that was their base, in the evenings, there would be up to a dozen scooters parked up, the Boys would spend the evening just talking about their machines, maybe fixing the latest accessory to make it look cool, things like leopards skin tails and flags tied to an aerial, springs to mind, and mirrors, the more mirrors the better, then all of a sudden, one or two of them would tear off up or down the high street, (they probably noticed a few girls) to show off to, I couldn't wait to be sixteen, as then I could get a bike licence.

About the same time as the birth of the scooter, the Japanese began to import motor bikes to England, and guess who was the first person in Cranbrook to have one, it was my old mate Deno, I was on my way home from work, as I got close to the Duke I could see someone outside sitting on a motor bike, it was Deno, already sixteen, sitting on his brand spanking new Honda Dream, it was like nothing I had ever seen, everything seemed so compact, the lights, indicators, dials, seat, wheels, were all so futuristic, and when I asked him to kick start it, he just pushed a button on the handle bars, and it roared into action, I've just seen the first electric start motor bike, shame it wasn't British, from that moment on, the British bike industry went into major decline, he let me sit on it, and said if I get a lid, he will take me for a spin, it goes without saying, it took no time at all too get one.

It was time to go home, and dream of having a machine just like Deno, sadly that would never happen. At least I had a job that was something, or was it? Everybody had a job in those days, Mr Burgess approached me one day, he said he would like me to go to the Institute of Butchers, where I would be trained to be a first class Butcher, and learn Management skills, something he really wanted me to do, I said I would think about it, but to be honest it was the idea of going back to school that put me off, in hind sight I should have given it more thought, but there you go, he continued to ask me the same question every now and again, in the end he gave up, I think he could tell I wasn't keen, when you think about it, Horace was prepared to lose me for a couple days a week, still pay my wages, he must have thought quite a lot of me, and perhaps saw more potential in me, than I could see myself.

I still continued to love my job, we were like a family, Mr Burgess wasn't in the best of health, he had gore stone problems which were apparently very painful, in the end he had to take time off to go to Hospital, to have them removed, I was now sixteen, old enough to buy a scooter or motor bike, only problem was I never had any money, but you could get higher purchase at certain dealers, the only place in our area was the bike dealer in Maidstone, I remember going there on the Bus, to see what they could do for me, by some pure luck the bike dealership was just opposite the bus station, in Knight Rider Street, I had a look round to see what was on offer, and the only bike that I could afford was a 250cc Francis Barnet, in horrible green, it was that or nothing, so I decided to go ahead and apply for higher purchase, the man got the forms out, filled in what he could, and said, because I was only sixteen, Mum had to sign it as well, so I had to take the form home, then post it back to the dealership, obviously Mum was reluctant to sign it, but I managed to talk her round, the form was sent off, all I had to do was wait for them to let me know, if I was successful or not, in those days things took time, I think it was something like three weeks before I got the ok, the big day arrived, off I went on the bus, to collect my first motor bike, a Fanny Barnet as it was called, it had no street cred whatsoever, the man in the dealership gave me instructions on how to start it, etc, I couldn't wait to get on that open road back home, I hadn't told him, but I had never rode a bike before, which was going to be interesting, I remember pulling away from the dealership totally out of control, but thankfully by the time I arrived home I was reasonably confident with myself, all the lads at Henniker came and had a look, David I think said something like, what do you want a bloody old thing like that for? I remember Mum popping out to see what I had purchased, she thought it was lovely, I think it was because it was a bit old fashioned and not too fancy.

The Boys asked me to take it up the road so they could watch me, so I kick started it, away she roared, from our front path it was a short steep climb to the pavement next to the road, I mounted my machine, pointed it up the steep inclimb, trying to let the clutch out slowly, something I hadn't perfected by a long chalk, needless to say I shot up the steep incline, shooting out into the road, then ending up in the ditch the other side, Mum was having kittens, imagine, seeing your son on a motorbike for the first time, then this sort of thing happens, fortunately I soon got the hang of it, before too long I was reasonably safe.

I only had my bike a few weeks, during the weekday evenings, we would congregate in the high street, some of us on motor bikes, some on push bikes, and the others on foot, on this particular evening, we were just standing about as normal passing the time away, when Ginger Briley joined us, now he was bad news, a right trouble maker, and only ever happy when he was beating someone up, he was drunk as usual, and still only sixteen, sadly all his life he was trouble, I believe he became reliant on drugs, and died at a very early age, I felt sorry for his family, anyway on this particular evening he asked me, if I would let him go for a spin on my bike, I of course said no, I thought that was the end of it, but he bided his time, waited until I wasn't looking, jumped on my bike and sped off up the high street, there wasn't much I could do about it, except wait for him to come back, we waited and waited, but no Ginger Briley, so no bike, sometime later, a copper rolled up and asked if anyone owned a Francis Barnet, I said yes and deep down knew he had an accident, apparently he had lost control along Angley Road, he was in a bad way, so they had taken him to the Kent and Sussex Hospital in Tunbridge Wells. My bike was a right off, so was Briley, well almost, his face looked like he had done ten rounds with Henry Cooper. My bike was only insured third party, so I had to pay for the repairs, which I couldn't afford, Briley said he would pay but never did, I was stuffed, I think we sold it back to the place I purchased it from, Mum got in touch with the HP company, to sort some sort of deal, I know I had still to pay for it, but with what they gave me for it, reduced the monthly payments, and that was it, I never bought another road bike ever again, I decided to stay with my push bike until I could afford a car.

By this time Mr Burgess seemed to be going downhill, during the next few weeks, there were a lot of comings and goings in the shop, Horace seemed to be talking to a lot of people, we were soon to find out, that he had decided, due to ill health, to put a Manager in the shop.

It all seemed to happen quite quickly, we were introduced to a Mr and Mrs Kennet, and their Son Mick, who were going to manage the shop, and live in the flat above. The Kennet's spent a couple of weeks with Mr and Mrs Burgess, to be shown the ropes; they seemed a very nice couple. Sadly their Son Mick was a different kettle of fish, I think he was about twenty, quite short, a bit tubby with long curly hair, a right cocky bugger, the girls thought he was lovely, the rumour was, he would take a girl out in his car, if they never gave him what he wanted, he would leave them there, he also owned a motorbike, it was a 750 Triumph Bonneville, probably the best around, it was light blue and silver, a proper racing machine, with clip on handle bars he offered to take me to Brands Hatch to watch a bike meeting, I of course jumped at the chance, we left quite early, it was a Sunday morning, and raining, only got as far as Goudhurst, Mick cranked the machine over to negotiate a left hand bend, the bike just slid away from us, it seemed to slide forever, we came to a standstill when it hit the curb, I was bouncing along, then as I hit the verge I bounced over one of those metal bar fences, that had sharp points at the top, it was a miracle I never landed on them, the only injury I sustained was a badly grazed hand, someone in the house opposite patched me up, Mike checked the bike over, then off we went to Brands Hatch, the route was Goudhurst, Paddock Wood, onto the A20, then up the hill to Brands, stopping at the famous Johnson's cafe just before Brands, that is where all the bike Boys would meet on a regular basis, a few would attempt the special run, a record would be put on the juke box, the object was to speed off as fast as you could, down the hill to the roundabout, then back up the hill to the cafe, before the record had stopped playing, apparently only a hand full of riders ever managed to do it, this run had claimed a number of deaths over the years, so they re-named the hill, Death Hill.

I enjoyed the bike meeting, even though my hand was very painful it had swollen up like a balloon, it was my first ever visit to Brands Hatch, little did I know that one day I would be racing there, and winning races myself.

I was very sad when the final day for Mr and Mrs Burgess had arrived, many of their customers had sent cards, which were hanging everywhere in the shop, lots had bought presents, I know Mrs Burgess had tears streaming down her face, and I'm sure Horace was tearful as well.

We cleared up as usual, shut up shop, Mr Burgess took us all in the back with Mrs Burgess, and I think they gave us a glass of sherry each, did a little speech saying all sorts of nice things. Gave us a big roast joint each and said cheerio, Bob took his apron off, and shook Mr Burgess and Mrs Burgess by their hands and left, Mr Burgess turned to me and said Son once you are out of your work clothes come upstairs and knock on the door, he asked me in, and that was the first time I had been back in his Flat since I went for my interview, He told me to sit down, and tried to explain why he was retiring and the reason for getting a Manager in, he then spoke about the Institute of Butchers he wanted me to attend, He asked me one more time, this time he explained why, it was simply because, he honestly believed that in a few years time I would be able to manage his shop, wow I never saw that coming, Mr Burgess said to think about, which I sure was going to. I thought about this opportunity all the time, but I just couldn't seem to get excited about it, so it was left on the back boiler, meanwhile I just continued to do my job with the new Manager, Derek Gurr had got himself a job at Wilkes's, so we quite often bumped into each other whilst on our rounds.

On my way home on Wed, half day closing, I would always pop in to see Mrs Courtman, at her Kent Weather boarded Chalet Bungalow, named Rosedene, just a few doors away from Henniker Cottages, we would chat for hours, drinking tea, eating cakes and sweets, if it was cold,

I can see it now, the fire would be roaring it's head off, Mrs Courtman would be sat on a wooden chair, skirt up past he knees, in front of the fire, you could see the inside of her legs getting redder and redder, nearly always I was still there when Mr Courtman came home from work, his remarks were the same every time, what's he doing here? At that time he never liked me, but Mrs Courtman thought the world of me, which was good, because I really wanted to go out with their Daughter Anne, but as yet no luck, I never realised but Mrs Courtman was quite ill, in fact it was cancer, and sadly she died at a very young age I think forty eight. she lost her battle very quickly, which was probably for the best. Brenda the oldest Daughter had just got Married. Hazel was still very young, so it was up to Anne to look after the house and her Dad etc, which was an almighty task at the tender age of fifteen. I do know poor Anne was going through a bad patch, I think it was a bit of a breakdown, as she didn't seem to be able to cope, let's face it, I don't think anyone could have coped, any better at that age or any age, So I decided not to bother her for a while, or it may have been Mum who suggested it.

Rosedene.

Most of my time was taken up by work, rushing home for a quick change, and something to eat, then it was out the door, to either the Corner Cafe, or Court Style Cricket ground, both had their interests, Court Style was somewhere to go and have fun messing about in the woods that separated the Cricket Ground from the main road, we also had a bike track that was fun, there were a few girls that used to hang around, one was a right goer, I recall at fourteen, she would jump in and out of the parked lorries, and service the drivers, but there were some nice girls there as well, one girl I took a shine too was Jenny Farmer, I don't believe I ever went out with her.

Then there was the Corner Cafe, I think the owners name was Vic, it was on the left, just as you entered Waterloo Road from Stone Street, almost opposite Windmill Hill Road, It hadn't been open that long, I think it may have been a Tea Room before that, but now it catered for us Teenagers which was great, the place was always full of youngsters, drinking pop and having one of their fabulous mushrooms and tomatoes on toast, toasted sandwiches, filled jacket potatoes or breakfast's, we would spend hours in there, the Boys from the Grammar School would often pop in as well, I often looked at them and imagined what it may have been like, if I had managed to go there, it was the place to catch up on all the gossip, at that time it was all about this girl that worked for Tim Brinton, he had purchased this big house at Willesley Pound, almost opposite the Willesley Hotel, at that time he was a news reporter on television, I think a bit later on, he may have also became a member of Parliament, she was a very well formed Girl, the only thing that let her down was her face, it must have been spotty, you would never see her without loads of makeup on, her whole face would be covered in something or other, but could still see all the spots, to be honest, we all stared at her but I'm sure, if everyone else was like me, we were all bloody terrified of her. Still it was all good fun.

That was the place to see all the characters like Charlie Burgess, known as Charlie Mole, a short hunched up Boy that was very insecure, when he was in the cafe, he would drink can after can of Pepsi, then make a point of being seen to crush the can with one hand, and to be fair, in those days the cans were much thicker than they are today, and not many of us could crush them like Charlie Mole, I certainly couldn't, he lived down Glastonbury Road, which was the road that went from the Tollhouse Stores Hartley, to the main Sissinghurst to Goudhurst road; it joined this road where the Peacock Pub was and still is today? His Dad was much older than his Mum,

I only ever went to his place once, he always seemed to yearn for friendship, but sadly nobody was interested, the last time I can remember seeing him, was one Saturday afternoon, he was walking down Stone Street, sucking on a roll up, I stopped to pass the time of day, asked how he was, he was very strange, he told me that the FBI or something like that were after him, so he hid his money and tobacco on his socks, it wasn't long after that he was admitted to Oakwood Mental Institute in Maidstone, then a while later we heard that he had hung himself, poor old Charlie.

Loads of us would meet up and pass the time of day, a chap named John Saunders that lived down Mead Road, Hartley, became a friend, he learnt to be a mechanic and proved very useful as time went by, he also had a younger Brother Derek, that had a motorbike, he was a complete nutter, and sadly killed himself, his Mum was devastated, and to make things worse her Husband had only just passed away as well, Mrs Saunders, was a big woman, I was terrified of her, a very loud Woman that always had a fag hanging out of her mouth, I think she was a chain smoker, she was very much like the Woman in the TV series George and the Dragon, Although we never became bosom buddies, I did get to know John well, and we certainly had some fun together, and it was a very sad occasion, when he died of leukaemia at the young age of thirty.

Most nights we would be in the Corner Cafe until they chucked us out, which was about eight thirty, Vic would say the same old thing, haven't you got any homes to go to? I have! So sod off.

It was about this time they had finished building the Mary Sheaf School for Girls, I was able to see the building progress every day, as I was out delivering on my trades bike, still being very young, the School Girls obviously interested me, the School was situated along Angley Road, laying well back from the road, with the ground being flat I could see very clearly what was going on, at that time the biggest single private housing estate was also under way, Wheatfield Way, the estate stretched from Angley Road all the way to Jockey Lane, which was just off the high street, I'm not sure how many houses exactly were built, but it must have been in the hundreds.

I don't know if there was any opposition, but for sure it probably changed Cranbrook forever, it must have been good for the Town, and good for employment.

Talking about employment, it was now common place to see the tradesmen and labourers, shopping in the town, eating in the cafes and drinking in the pubs, the White Horse was the favourite, I guess because it was the nearest.

The White Horse. My favourite dinking hole when I was a Lad. Jockey Lane is to the right.

Before too long opportunities arose with vacancies for labourers, mainly for bricklayers and plasterers, one of the first to apply was my friend Derek Gurr, he got a job for a Plastering company that won the contract for this site, the money he was earning was unbelievable, I thought I want some of that, and as soon as there was a vacancy I went and applied for it, I must admit when I went to the site to apply for the job, I felt out of my depth, bearing in mind I was still such a little fellow, and when you get on a site that's full of these big hairy arsed labourers, you feel intimidated, I saw the hod carriers run up planks, then tipping up there Hods of bricks, Derek was there, mixing up sand and cement at the time, he looked as if he knew what he was doing, so I thought if he can do it then so can I.

Derek took me to the Boss, Frank Lockyer, he was a larger than life type of bloke, loved to take the piss, which he did, he asked me a few questions, then if I remember correctly, got me to carry a bag of cement, which was a hundred weight in those days, the trick was to pick it up in your arms then throw it onto your shoulder, no chance, I also had to fill and carry a plasterers hod, which is twice the size of a bricklayers hod when you get used to it, if you load it correctly, it is possible to get a full barrow load of pug in that hod. I got the job, god knows how, he said I could start whenever I wanted,, I now had to go and see Mr Kennet, to hand in my notice, this proved much easier that I thought, he had an idea, I could be leaving, and although he was upset, he wished me good luck.

So seventeen and a career move, I wondered if I had made the right decision, all sorts of things were going through my head; would it be too hard for me? Would Horace be annoyed, I suppose in a way I was his prodigy, and in answer to those questions, yes it was bloody hard, harder than I could ever had imagined, and was he upset, yes he dam well was.

I told Mr Kennet on the Thursday, he was good enough to let me go on the Saturday, so my new job began on the Monday, at Wheatfield Way.

By more luck than judgement, I was broken in quite gently, I arrived on time, in fact I was the only one there, but before long they drifted in, Derek was next, then the plasterers, Frank Lockyer his Brother Fred, Alec Galloway and Peter Batten, they arrived in a car driven by Frank, as I think about it now, they all had their own strange habits, Frank would do a lot of blinking, Fred would always be twitching the side of his face, Alec would have this habit of squeezing the sides of his body, as if he was trying to pull his trousers up with his elbows, Peter Batten never had any strange habits, he just looked strange, he was a giant of a Man, with hands as big as dinner plates, and big bulging eyes, that appeared to be popping out of his head, but strangely enough, he had the smallest mouth I think I have ever seen on someone that large, fancy seeing that lot coming towards you in a dark alley?

I think my first day was cleaning one of the houses out, after it had been plastered, it was filthy, all the rendering that had been left on the floor had gone rock hard, it was a right mess, I decided when I was labouring for real, I would clean up the same day, mind you I soon found out how difficult that will be, the Plasterers or Spreads as they are known would plaster till the last minute, then wash their tools, then go home, I think maybe because they were short of labourers they probably did it themselves, so when the last bit of rendering or plaster was finished, they said sod it and went home, leaving it in right old mess, I decided because I lived local, and had my own push bike, it seemed sensible for me to stay after they went home, to clear up, it was an extra hour but so much better to arrive in the morning all clean and tidy, they were well impressed, and when it came to skimming the ceilings, I would stay late the night before, sheet the rooms out with scaffold boards to the correct height, ready for the morning, it made life so much easier, it was hard enough as it was, although I was completely knackered, I really enjoyed being a plasterers labourer, we worked hard, but had loads of fun, I soon begun to know when one of them was in a bad mood, Frank would lose it and not care, Peter would sulk for days, Alec would slowly get wound up then smash everything in sight, and Fred, he was always the same, don't think I ever saw him in a bad mood, he just twitched that little bit quicker.

In those days the spreads would get forty five pounds to plaster a house, which included skimming the ceilings, render and setting the walls and laying a sand and cement screed to the ground floor.

We had to do two houses a week, the first coat on the walls was sand and cement, which I knocked up by hand, no mixer in those days, it wasn't unusual to knock up a ten ton lorry load of sand with cement, and carry it in to the house in a day.

After a week's graft I always looked forward to Friday nights, still only sixteen but we would all meet in the White Horse, and drink ourselves silly, my favourite tipple was rum and blackcurrant, until I got so ill on the stuff, It put me right off and haven't touched a drop since, then it was on the ninety seven bus to Hawkhurst, back into a pub at the top of the hill, to down more of the same, then just up the road to the village hall's Friday night dances, every week there would be a band of some description, and they were very good, one in particular, Dave Champion and the Strangers comes to mind, most times I was so drunk I never had a clue what was going on, and for whatever reason, I would always get into a fight, and get knocked about, maybe I was a bit leery or perhaps it was because I was an easy target being drunk and small, I also recall wearing this black leather jacket, which I wore to work as well, it would clean it up with black boot polish for my nights out, it looked great, but the only problem was, if I was lucky enough to grab a girl, and have a dance, her dress would end up covered in black boot polish, never mind eh?

1962 and we were about to enter the worst winter England had for years, it snowed and snowed almost continuously, the ice was packed on the pavements and roads as hard as concrete, I had only been in the job a few months then due to the bad weather I was out of work, but to be fair Frank was very helpful, he would give me the odd job to do, at his bungalow in Tenterden, in return for a few bob, some of the jobs were awful I remember him having a frozen pipe, I had to break through his path to get to the pipe, I was absolutely bloody freezing, sometimes when Derek and myself went over for a sub, which he would deduct off any wages we may get, he got us to box against each other in his front room, the winner got the cash for nothing, the other one got the cash, but had to pay it back, I was surprised as I expected Derek to win, he was much bigger than me, but nine times out of ten I was the winner, that's when I discovered, the bully I knew at school, was just a great big woos, on one occasion I actually knocked him out, Frank was over the moon, however his wife, went crackers, and stopped it, so no more fights for money.

The big freeze continued until April, and what a relief when it was all over, in the meantime, we just bummed around, if we had any cash, sometimes would take a trip to Staplehurst, there would be a few of us and most of the time we managed to grab someone with a car, our place of call was the station cafe, situated down a road that led to Staplehurst Railway Station, we would have the radio blearing out with the hits of that time, Elvis Presley was the main Man, the record I can remember the most was, return to sender, at the cafe we would play table football, which was very popular, the cafe owner a bit of a wide Boy, had two Daughters, can't remember their names, but they were unbeatable at table football, we soon discovered never to play them for money, as you would never win, it was a great place to waste time, after all we had plenty of that.

As the weather cleared we were hoping Frank would get in touch, and to be fair he did just that, he said once he gets the ok to start back we would be the first to know, so the moment the site Foreman at Wheatfield Way gave Frank the nod we were back in collar, it had been well over four months, couldn't wait to get back to earn some money.

Work started to come in left right and centre, Frank and Fred were earning a small fortune, Frank loved to spend, I remember it wasn't too long before he had got himself a new car, it was a Mark ten Jaguar, wow, Fred was more prudent, he seemed quite happy letting Frank be the front Man, he could sweet talk anyone, plus I'm sure he gave the odd drink here and there to the right people.

Before too long quite a few of the Tradesmen and Labourers bought a house at Wheatfield Way, Frank already had his bungalow at Tenterden, Fred, Alec and Peter Batten all bought one, at that time you could buy a brand new semi for between two thousand five hundred and three thousand pounds.

Also the mini came out, I remember Frank rolling up with a brand new Mini Van, I think it cost about three or four hundred pounds. Work was good, money was coming in, and the world seemed to be our Lobster's.

Phase one of Wheatfield Way was completed, until they had phase two ready, we moved further afield, it was to be Langton Green just the other side of Tunbridge Wells, it was a small development of about twenty executive houses, big five bedroom places with on suite, family bathroom, fully fitted kitchen's and big double garages, we didn't have to do two of these a week, that's for sure, and the finish had to be spot on, something Peter and Alec weren't used too, for me it was quite an adventure travelling all that way to work, I think petrol in old money was four and eleven pence a gallon, that's less than fifty pence.

Chapter 5.
The girl for me- pregnancy and marriage

Now I was seventeen, Alec told me to get a driving licence, they would then allow me to drive the van to work, things were getting better and better, it wasn't long before I got my first car, a three year old Hillman Minx, two tone, coffee and cream, now I was unstoppable, I went everywhere, although even with petrol at that price I found it bloody hard to afford , my friend John Saunders, had just purchased a car too, and it was a Hillman Minx, what a coincidence, with John being a car mechanic, it was brilliant, if anything needed doing, John would do it, for a packet of fags, he loved his fags just like his Mum, we started to venture a little bit out of our area, mainly to Pembury and Tunbridge Wells, as we heard there were plenty of (birds) girls available out that way, one evening as we were cruising through the high street of Tunbridge Wells, we spotted a couple of birds hanging around outside the Cinema, after driving past and waving, we got a response, so decided to pull over for a chat, we got on with them ok, so we went for a spin in our cars, I had a girl called Ann, we got on well, when it was time to go, we asked them if we could drop them off at their homes, they said yes, and with that I asked her if she would like to see me again, she said she would, so I made arrangements to see her in a few days, which I did, I would go and see Ann on a regular basis, although I still only had a provisional licence, in those days you could get away with it, however the girl I wanted to really go out with, was Anne Courtman, the girl that lived just a few doors away, she was different and very special, I kept pestering her to come out with me, but no luck, at the time she was going out with a chap from smarden, his name was Dennis Bridgland, I would even run him home when he visited Anne, basically to keep in her good books, then one day she said that she would go out with me, I think the first time was with John Saunders in his car, he had his girlfriend in the front, so I sat in the back with Anne, I don't think it was so much a date as we were taking Anne to see her friend Sue Ralph, that lived in Four Throws, just before Hawhurst, but I do remember my first ever snogg, it was just after Tubs lake, I decided to take a chance and try, she responded, fantastic, my first kiss with the girl I really wanted.

Naturally I tried to take her out again, she knew I had a girlfriend, and also was aware I didn't have a full driving licence, but she did say!, pass your test, and tell your girlfriend you don't want to see her anymore, then I will go out with you, I will not two time, I very quickly passed my test, told my girlfriend I wanted to finish it, then went back and told Anne, I could get her attention quite easily as I parked my car in a lay-by opposite her house, I had everything crossed, she said yes, I can tell you this was the best moment of my life.

My biggest concern was to convince Mr Courtman that I was good enough to go out with his Daughter. I had to appreciate the fact, that Anne was the one that had to look after her Dad and younger Sister Hazel, since her Mum died, so that was priority, we couldn't go gallivanting everywhere, if we did go out, she had to be back by nine o'clock, as soon as I parked my car in the lay by, Anne's Dad would be by the car saying, nine o'clock Anne, in you come, a bit of a pain, but I didn't mind, and Mum was over the moon, she really liked Anne.

Mum was still having grief from Johnny Boy, one day I was with Anne at Rosedene, when I think it was Eileen looking very tearful and distressed, asked for me, she said Johnny Boy was threatening Mum, with that I shot back home, and warned him, if he as much as laid a finger on her I would kill him, I got in touch with the police, they said unless he actually harms her there is nothing they can do, talk about the Law being an Ass, thankfully, by now, Johnny Boy was no more than a lodger, I never really spoke to him, I suppose because I had a proper girlfriend, I was able to spend lots of time at Rosedene, and keep out of his way, I do believe Mr Courtman was beginning to accept the fact that I was serious about Anne, so slowly, slowly, I started to win him round.

When Anne left School she worked as a Nanny for Friday's, the chicken egg suppliers, after that it was London

Outfitters in Cranbrook, which is situated right opposite the White Horse, I don't believe she worked there for long, she had too many responsibilities at home looking after things. Anne's Dad, became friendly with someone he knew that lived in Smarden, she was a lovely Lady, by the name of Bet, a real old fashioned type of Mum, Anne and Hazel, liked her too, she, would visit a couple of times a week, and always have a bag of goodies, and some, homemade pies mmmmm. I would nearly always take her home; Anne came with me which was nice. Bet was a very understanding Lady, if we had any worries; we knew we could go to her.

I was now beginning to get to grips with plastering, in those days the labourer was expected to carry out certain tasks to help the plasterers, one was to devil up the walls that have just been rendered, this was going over the walls that had just been rendered with a flat piece of wood with a handle, it had small nails poking out of the top edge, the idea was to put scratch marks on the render, to give it a grip ready to take the finished plaster coat, known as the scim coat, as time progressed, I was trusted with actually plastering the cupboards, the one under the stairs was a nightmare, but it was all a good learning curve, I seemed to get the hang of it fairly quickly, and on one occasion I managed to get Alec and Peter to allow me to render the outside of a garage, at a job near Tunbridge, I would take my own car to work, then stay and put the rendering on, rush home, pick Anne up then go back, finish it off the best I could, then get Anne home by Nine o'clock, I even remember what Anne would wear, most of the time it was a pair of those black tight jogging bottoms with a light blue jumper.

My spare time naturally was with Anne, we often visited her sister Brenda and her Husband Bernard, they lived in Tunbridge Wells, I can remember Bernard when he was courting Brenda, he would get off the bus and walk down to Rosedene, at that time he had a mass of black hair and looked a right hard nut, so we never said anything to him, actually he is quite the opposite.

I also enjoyed visiting Anne's Grandparents that live in the arms house at the Moor Hawkhurst, her Gran was a tiny little Lady, whilst her Granddad was a big burley chap, they reminded me of the Grandparents in the Walton's, what lovely people they were, and still sorely missed.

Anne's Grandparents. With Mrs Courtman, Brenda-Anne-Hazel

I seemed to be turning into a reasonably stable sort of person, but thankfully never lost that sparkle or cheekiness.

Things at home were not good, but Mum managed on the odd occasion to go out and enjoy herself, it was about this time when she told me that she had met someone she really like, and would love me and Anne to meet him, I said yes no problem, Mum arranged to meet this guy at Staplehurst, it was suggest we met up at the Railway Tavern, which is on the main road out of Staplehurst opposite the road that leads to the Railway Station.

When we arrived he was already there, he was a tall thin Man, in a dark coat and a white silk scarf, Mum introduced us, his name was Leonard, he was very charming, I could tell Mum was smitten by him, and I was delighted for her, we sat in the pub all evening, until it was time for him to catch his train, he lived in London, had his own house, a good job, and it seemed plenty of money, on our way home we were all excited, it was just as if Mum had won the pools, and it was fantastic to see that sparkle back, he was a very generous Man, he wouldn't let us buy a thing, we took Mum to meet him several times, we went us to all sorts of places, mainly really good restaurants, even some in London, including the Lyons Corner House, we also used to go to the Bamboo Sky in Hastings, it had this amazing waterfall, that would thunder and lightning towards the end of the night, they did a great minute steak, that would be cooked at the table, my goodness we were having a lovely time. Anne and I felt very happy together, I had no doubt, that she was the girl for me, so I asked her if she would like to get engaged, she said yes, but felt I had better ask her Dad's permission, so I did and thank the Lord he said yes. I was over the moon.

Not long after us getting engaged, Mum told me Leonard has asked her to marry him, bloody hell, I thought great, but does he really know what he is taking on.

I was now nineteen and very settled, I was doing well with the plastering, Frank asked me if I would like to go on the tools fulltime, naturally I jumped at the chance, he told me to find myself a labourer, which I did, it was Peter Giles, the son of Mrs Giles, the Lady that looked after Chris, Peter, and Eileen. He was a good worker, but a bit quiet, I felt so grown up, being a plasterer and having my own labourer, things continued to be good

I would pop in to see Anne on my way home from work, on this occasion she had been crying, I asked her what the problem was, she said that she was pregnant, and didn't know what to do, I must admit, neither did I.

I think the first thing we did was tell my Mum, she must have asked all the questions to Anne, including how many weeks pregnant etc, I think she advised us not to panic, but wait a couple of weeks then decide, the couple of weeks came and went, and it was clear, Anne was definitely pregnant, we knew we had to tell Anne's Dad, I really wasn't looking forward to this.

I suggested that when Bet comes over next, we take her home, and explain what has happened, Bet arrived, we tried to be as normal as we could, knowing that we were about to drop a bombshell on her later.

The evening flew by, it was soon time to take Bet home, we knew that this was the best time to tell her, but we were both so terrified to say something, anyway, I think it must have been me that started to explain things, Anne was tearful, Bet listened, and said something like, these things happen, and believe me, Andrew (Anne's dad) and I have had a few near misses, I think she just said that to make us feel a bit better, Bet decided that she would tell Andrew the news, in a couple of days time, when she was over again, so in the meantime say nothing, Anne and myself were shitting ourselves, with the knowledge that Anne's Dad would erupt. Two days later Bet arrived as promised, Bet told us to stay in the front room, whilst she had a chat with Andrew in the back room, we could hear Bet talking to Anne's Dad, He was devastated, and to be fair I can now understand how he must have felt, having just lost his wife, Brenda was just married, and Anne was his rock in many ways, then I come along and messed things up, plus he told Anne a while ago, I don't mind who you go out with, but you're not going out with that Rick Shortle, it was a right bugger, as I was just beginning to win him round, then this happens, I certainly had some work to do, to prove I was not as bad as he thought,

Sadly this wasn't the end of this announcement, Andrew was in shock, he said he intends to ask his Sister Kate over, to help sort this mess out, I can remember it vividly, Bet, bless her came over to prepare tea, Auntie Kate arrived, I kept a low profile, she never spoke to me, we were all summons to the table, and the moment we sat down Auntie Kate blurted out, how dare you do this to Andrew, after everything he has done for you, or something like that, I just exploded, probably because that was the only way I could cope with the situation, I'm not sure what happened after that, but one thing was for sure, I didn't get any brownie points for my behaviour.

I did apologise for my outburst, I felt as if I wanted to run away and hide, I couldn't wait for Auntie Kate to leave, but that wouldn't be until the following day, Sunday, although Anne was annoyed with my outburst, she too was surprised at the way Auntie Kate tried to sort things out, Bet as always was fantastic, a very understanding wise Lady.

Anne and I decided to carry on and get engaged, apart from the fact she was pregnant, we were in love, so we would have got in engaged, anyway, we had a long chat about the future, and decided to get married as soon as we possibly could, we discussed it with Ann's Dad and he agreed, the sooner the better, unfortunately, he wasn't going to allow a Church Wedding, as he felt it would be wrong, considering the circumstances, in those days people like Andrew had strong beliefs, so we had to respect his wishes, I do know Anne has always regretted not being married in a church with all the trimmings, maybe one day, I will surprise her, and have a blessing in the church.

So we decided to go ahead, and organise a date at the Maidstone Registry Office, the earliest date was the 02/10/1965, I never had much in the way of savings, so the start of our marriage certainly wasn't going to be fairytale wedding, but that didn't matter.

I decided to try and top up my earnings, by working all the hours that God made, at that time we were working at West Kingsdown, not far from Brands Hatch, a bit of a journey so we would leave home at four in the morning, in those days I was a bugger for getting up, so I tied a piece of thread to my toe, then dangled the thread out of the window, Peter would arrive in the morning and if the thread was still hanging he would give it a tug to wake me up, it worked perfectly. Frank Lockyer was fine with what I was doing; I tried not to draw too much money off the job until just before the wedding, which was mounting up very nicely.

We were going to hold the reception at Rosedene, as it was only going to be a small family affair, on my side just Mum and Leonard, on Anne's side, her Dad, Bet, Brenda, Husband Bernard, and Hazel now thirteen, I wasn't annoyed about the fact it was such a small affair, I was over the moon I was getting married, and not for a moment did I think, here I am, barely twenty, getting married with a baby on the way.

I worked right up until the day before the wedding, to earn as much as I possibly could, Alec was now the person that brought the wages round, the plastering business was going from strength so Frank wasn't doing much, just counting his money, Alec arrived, looking a bit sheepish, I knew something was up, he explained to me, my plastering was not up to standard, and I was not being paid, I was devastated, all that hard work, for nothing, I know for a fact my plastering was ok, it was something they had done before to other sub-contractors another way of making money, but to do it to me was absolutely disgusting, so there I was, the day before my wedding, not a pot to piss in, no wonder I look so bloody miserable in the wedding photo.

Going back a tad, Mum and Leonard had decided to get married, it was going to be a week before ours, Mum had planned her escape away from Johnny Boy, which was basically to take just her clothes, and the kids of course, the plan was to stay at Leonards Sister's in Hastings, until he was organised enough to take everyone to his house in Earlsfield near Tooting London, I can remember Mum doing a runner before Johnny Boy came home, I don't think for a moment he was bothered, after all, he was left with No Three Henniker Cottages fully furnished, what Johnny Boy did after that I haven't a clue, Mum got Married in the Hastings Registry Office, I was sleeping on site for the week leading up to our wedding, it was much too far to travel, after the news I wouldn't be paid, I decided to go home, no point in working, Alec and Peter Batten had the ordacity to ask if I would like to go for a celebratory drink, (Bastards).

I felt sick and didn't know what to do, I had a few quid, and that was it, I decided to make out all was ok, how could I tell Anne what had happened? I couldn't we were getting married tomorrow. I dropped Peter Giles off without all his money, luckily it was only the last few days he was owed, as I would always draw enough to pay him each week, he was very good about it, he knew what they were up to, in hindsight I should have drawn up tight each week for myself as well.

The journey home to Hastings seemed never ending, and Boy was I glad to get there, Leonard's Sister, Lilly, had a lovely three story Georgian House not far from the sea, very grand, in fact to us it was a bloody palace. It was arranged Anne and I would have the top floor flat that was available; at least we had one piece of luck, our own place, no money but our own place.

Saturday morning, up early, as I wanted to clean my car, this was the big day, my car was parked just up the road as there wasn't any room outside the house, I jumped in to move it nearer, started it up, drew away, no brakes, thinking it probably needed topping up with brake fluid, I checked it and it was low, dear oh dear, that's all I need the morning of my Wedding day, I shot off on foot to the local garage to get some brake fluid, topped it up, but found that it was leaking like crazy from one of the pipes, I couldn't do anything about that, I tried to find some local mechanic to fix it, without luck, time was running out, we had to be at Maidstone, so I made a decision, that I would drive from Hastings to Maidstone, then Maidstone to Hartley, then Hartley to Hastings, without any bloody brakes, Mum and Leonard, agreed, I don't think they quite understood what was wrong, all I had was the handbrake, driving like this was a nightmare, unfortunately it made me late for my own wedding, but thankfully we arrived safe and sound, and praise to the Lord the registrar waited, not doing very well with the perfect Husband points was I?

Feeling slightly up tight, but over the moon I have just married the girl of my dreams, looking so radiant, although Anne was five months pregnant it didn't show at all, it was now all back to Rosedene for the reception, Bet as usual had cast her magic, she had laid on a lovely spread, the weather was good, everyone seemed happy for us, I think I was the only one to find it difficult to smile, simply because I knew what was going on, and that I had to tell my new Wife the truth, but for now I tried to act as if all was well. We had a few photo's taken in Andrew's back garden, listened to a couple of speeches, we were given some presents, and thankfully some cash as well, I think in total about twenty five pounds, which was quite a lot in those days, probably a good two weeks wages, which made me a bit more relaxed, I had a couple of weeks to hopefully find another job.

Our Wedding photo, try to smile Rick

Wedding reception over, we now had to load the car up with all Anne's belongings, presents etc, I can remember the car being so full that we had nowhere to put what was left of the wedding cake, so that went on the roof in a box along with lots of other bits and pieces. We said our goodbyes, got in the car and pulled away, we hadn't gone that far when I looked in the mirror to see the wedding cake fly off the roof, it hit the road and went everywhere; it wasn't worth stopping, so we kept jogging along to Hastings.

I'm not sure if I told Anne about the brakes, she thinks I may have done, but I don't think I did, anyway we made it Hastings, and our new home. I told Anne that I will be having a few days off.

So the pressure was off for a short while, and for a few days everything seemed surreal, we were so happy, spent most of the time being silly, I would dress up like the Hunch Back of Notre dame, to frighten Anne, just be altogether daft and without a care in the world, however reality was just around the corner.

That inevitable day had arrived, I couldn't keep away from work any longer, I knew that I should tell Anne that I didn't have any money, or a job, for a couple of days I couldn't bring myself to tell her, so I made out I was going to work, after a couple of days, I was courageous enough to explain the whole thing. I was so relieved it was out in the open, by that time, Leonard had decided to take us all to live in his house in London, which was a good idea, as Hastings is and always has been a difficult place to find work, I think Lilly was glad to see the back of us anyway, so within a few days we were all packed and ready to go.

Chapter 6:
London Bound.

I don't think I had ever been to London, apart from the odd visit to Lions Corner House etc with Mum and Leonard, neither had the rest of the gang, Leonards directions were crap, he didn't have a clue how to get there, but in the end we arrived at Earlsworth road, Earlsfied, London. Leonard's house was one in a row; it was three stories high, and extremely tidy. I remember being greeted by a woman called Mrs Par, she lived on the top floor, and although she was aware that Leonard had a Lady friend, I'm not sure if she knew he had just got married, I remembering her pulling him to one side, and asking him if he had explained about his Son Barry.

The rest of the day was spent bringing stuff in from the car, sorting out who would sleep where, Peter in particular was still very young, but so was Chris and Eileen, unfortunately on the very first day one or two china pieces got broken, by these three little devils, Leonard was quite ok about it, but he very quickly moved everything of value, to a safe haven, didn't blame him with us lot around.

Leonard must have explained something to Mum, because she said that she needed to tell us something, what Leonard hadn't told Mum was, he had a twenty year old Son called Barry, that had Down's Syndrome, I suppose I can understand him being nervous about telling Mum, he probably thought if she knew, that would be the end, although it was a shock, we all accepted the fact, and had many happy times with Barry, he was an expert on football, he supported Fulham and I don't think there was anything he didn't know. About his beloved Football Team

It took a while to settle in, and even more importantly, time for Leonard to get over the culture shock, by now Anne was six months pregnant, and we were told by Mum, that she was three months pregnant as well, in fact it turned out to be perfect, Mum a seasoned Mother, would be visiting the hospital with Anne, and doing all the usual things Mum's to be do, it was comforting to know they would be doing all this together, how fortunate was that?

Priority for me was to find a job, so I scanned the local rag, Airfix were advertising for people, they are the famous model kit company, their construction and distribution centre was in Earlsfied just a walk away. I called them and was asked to pop in to see them, I went along straight away, the factory was a dire looking place, it was pretty big and ran parallel to the river Wandle, my interview took no time at all, I got the job, and got an immediate start, my initial job was working down stairs where all the kits were stacked ready for distribution, everything here was under ground, the only thing between us and the river Wandle was a road that allowed the trucks to drive down, so they could back onto to the loading bays, when it rained continuously it wasn't unusual to see us flooded, it was very claustrophobic the ceiling was hardly six feet high, I was fortunate being short. The building was massive, at least as big as a football pitch, from one end to the other was a dead straight walkway, about six feet wide, all the models were stacked either side in the alphabetical order, it took forever to remember where each kit was, but like most things it came with time, about three quarters of the way down, you could turn right along another path that lead to the underflow, this place was heaven if you were a lazy bugger, it was were all the kits that never saw light of day, because nobody wanted them were, the few guys that worked there seemed to do bugger all, from the time they started work to the time they finished, and nothing was ever done about it, I recon they were the foreman's hanger on's, they would spend all day playing cards and moaning about the wage being so bad, while the rest of us were working our nuts off, mind you I preferred to be working as the day passes by so much faster.

The job was very simply, I soon became a Charge hand, which not only gave me a bit more money, but allowed me to jump in the articulated lorries that required unloading, I had to back them onto the loading bay, which proved a very difficult exercise, but like all things you soon get used to it, we then unloaded the kits which were in tea chests.

Halfway down was the export division, it was run by I think four Caribbean's, this division was without doubt the most colourful, I've' never seen anything quite like it, and when they got going they would argue for hours, even wave knifes at each other, none of us ever knew what they were saying as it certainly wasn't English, and for whatever reason they were never disciplined, all this to me was completely new, I was so intrigued with it all.

I remember on one occasion, we had a bit of time to spare, we ended up messing about with a ball, one of the guys that worked alongside us by the name of Peter, he was a bit backward, but a really nice bloke, all the way along the walk way were lights, enclosed in small square glass cases, I can still see Peter to this day running along to catch a ball, forgetting how low the ceiling was, he must have jumped up or something, because his head caught the edge of one of the glass light cases, and took the flesh off the top of his head, it was awful. There was blood everywhere, fortunately the skin was still partly intact, and lucky for Peter he was bald, as it was to make things much easier to sow the flesh back on in the hospital, the Manager got the first aid man down, and decided he needed to be taken to hospital, I volunteered to take him, do you know he never once complained, if that was me I would be screaming the house down, Peter recovered quite quickly, and I think the authorities felt it was not the place to employ someone like Peter, which was a shame, he was sorely missed.

Anne was now almost nine months pregnant, we decided to go to the cinema and watch Rasputin the mad Monk,

I don't know if it was the film, that may have brought the birth on, but I think she began to sense something, that the birth of our baby was imminent, Anne made it through the night, it was either a Saturday or Sunday, I was doing overtime, and was hoping nothing would happen till I got home, as I was working the Security Man came and found me, he said that Anne had gone into labour and that she was in the Weir Hospital in Balham.

I was allowed to go, I remember clearing the gate with ease, on the way out of Air fix, I rushed to the Hospital, hoping I would get there in time, which I did, in those days, you were not allowed to go in the delivery room, so I said a few words of comfort just before she was wheeled into the delivery room.

This was all new to me, still only twenty, Anne only eighteen, baby due anytime, and at about three o'clock in the afternoon, our beautiful baby daughter was born, she was two weeks premature, and so tiny, that is why we called her Tina, wow I'm a Dad

Leonard was brilliant he sorted us out with our own room, as up till then we had been sleeping in the dining room, by putting a mattress on the floor, which wasn't ideal, we had a downstairs loo, situated outdoors, which meant the only way to get there, was through the dining room through the kitchen, out the back door, Barry slept downstairs, and every night he would go to the loo, we dreaded it, he would step across us with his dangly bits barely inches away ugh! So having a baby brought its rewards, Anne and I had our own bedroom, it was in fact part of the lounge that was divided with French doors, so we gained a bedroom and everyone else unfortunately ended up with a small lounge, still we managed.

Mum and Anne got on like a house on fire, they had so much in common, and when Mum had her baby, which was also Girl, named June, they would go out shopping, with their babies, having a great time, the strange bit was, June was Tina's Auntie, but June was younger than Tina, (I think that's correct).

We would try to go back to Kent as often as we could, to visit Anne's Dad and family, I must admit, we were so grateful to Leonard for looking after us, but the pull back to Kent was getting too tough to ignore.

Whilst we were down Kent visiting, I bumped into Alec Galloway of Tenterden and Cranbrook Plastering, we had a chat, and asked if I would be interested in coming back, I said I would think about it, and although I was still very upset about what they did to me, the day before I got married, this would be the way back to Kent, I spoke to Anne about the offer, we both agreed that we would be much happier back where we belong, so decided to move back to Kent, plus it would free up Leonards house, making things much more comfortable for everyone else.

We explained it to Andrew (Anne's Dad) he was over the Moon, it would make things so much easier for him and Hazel. So that was it, we were on our way back to

Rosedene, when we got back to London we told Mum and Leonard, and to be fair I think they were relieved, David had got a job at Airfix, Christopher, Eileen and Peter were settled, so all was fine.

I handed my notice in, Airfix were disappointed but allowed me to finish at the end of the week, and so back to Kent we go in six days time.

Although Anne and I enjoyed our time in London, we were so happy to be going back to Kent.

Chapter 7.
Back home

I can remember our journey from London, in those days, the M25 was just a twinkle in someone's eye, as we got ever nearer to Cranbrook, the scenery changed, initially never ending rows of terraced houses, followed by London Towns, blending into the next London Town, no rest bite or sight of open spaces.

That was until we got past Mitcham, from then on in it started to show signs of open countryside, and once we reached Westerham we were in the country, Sevenoaks. Pembury, then a few miles down the road, just after a copse of Eucalyptus trees on the right that had just been planted, they are still there to this day, but now they tower above everything else, you would turn left at the AA Box, signposted Goudhurst, in those days you would see an AA Man there with his motor bike, if you were a member and had the AA badge, he would salute. Imagine that today.

Once on the Goudhurst road the view is positively stunning, even to this day I am awestruck with its beauty, the road meanders its way towards Goudhurst, dropping down quite dramatically, past the hopper huts, that sadly are no longer in use, Hop Picking had died out, but it is a lovely reminder of days gone by, at the foot of the hill, you cross the river Teise, another reminder of when we were Kids, a favourite place to swim and fish, once over the river, there is a dwelling right on the river bank named Toad Hall, what a great name, as kids we thought it was the actual Toad Hall, past the garage on the right, then it's a long, long, climb to Goudhurst, and in a car then, it was a second gear job, especially the last bit, the trick was to get a good run from the bottom, don't lift, then it was fine, the view from here must equal anything, you can see the rolling hills for miles. And the people that live in the council estate at the top have a view to die for. Through Goudhurst, it's so quaint, with the pub and village pond right in the middle of the village, that was then, but today it's been ruined by all the traffic and people that park their cars in the high street, even on the pavement, god knows how pedestrians manage, nothing is ever done about it, I suppose they are more concerned with the revenue these people bring, rather than keeping it a natural place of interest and beauty, after all there is a perfectly adequate car park just behind the village pond, grrrrrrrrrrrr.

Not far now, as you leave the village, still climbing, the road is so very tight with an S bend at the top, it follows the Church wall which is right against the road; Goudhurst Church sits right at the top of the hill, in a commanding manner. A couple of miles further, turn right at the Peacock Pub, into Glastonbury road, go past where Charlie Mole used to live, carry on to the end of the road. Then turn left at the Tollhouse Stores, and barely before you had selected fourth gear, we had arrived at Rosedene, back to our own stamping ground.

The feeling of arriving and being back where we belonged was great, Anne's Dad was delighted, it wasn't long before Anne got to grips with taking care of things, we spent the first few days visiting, then it was back plastering, it was as if we had never been away, good job I had kept my tools.

Things just carried on quite normal, our daughter Tina was getting into everything, being spoilt rotten by Dad and Bet, I was busy plastering working in Biddenden, on a new housing estate named Spinners Close, it was a small development of about thirty houses, built in blocks of four, and very spacious They were up for sale from three thousand two hundred and fifty pounds, to four thousand two hundred and fifty pounds for the end of terrace, prices in 1968 were a tad lower than they are today, still all relative as they say, to us that was an awful lot of money. I visited the show house and had a chat with the Salesman, he explained that there was a special offer, providing I was earning enough, I would be granted a mortgage, and the developers would pay the deposit, so when I got home I spoke to Anne and Anne's Dad, it was a resounding yes, so all I had to do was to ask Frank Lockyer, if he would confirm my earnings. Frank obliged, so off we went to buy our first house and a brand spanking new one at that. We picked our plot and just had to wait for it to be built, I think we had to wait about three months before we moved in, it seemed like eternity, as with most first time buyers we couldn't afford furniture, so we relied on handouts from the family, for which we were most grateful.

You know what they say, new house new Baby, well right on queue Anne was pregnant, and on August 15th 1968 we were blessed with another lovely girl, we named her Julia, I was working in Bexhill at the time, Anne got someone to call the site, I was told she was taken to Kench Hill Hospital Tenterden, and that Mother and Baby were doing well, Anne couldn't wait to get home, but in those days, Mother and Baby were in Hospital for almost a week.

Andrew and Bet would visit every Wednesday, I recon it was to make sure Anne was ok, although I was getting on ok with Andrew I could tell he still had his reservations about me, it was going to take another ten or so years before he would totally accept me, I can now fully understand how he felt. Anne adapted to marriage without any problem whatsoever, but I still wanted to go out on a Friday night with my mates, have a few, or more than a few drinks, then drive home three sheets to the wind, thank the lord the breathalyser wasn't invented then, I have to put my hands up and admit I was quite a selfish person, and what's more we couldn't afford it anyway.

Unfortunately I was the sort of person that wouldn't worry too much about money, and found it extremely difficult to make sure we had enough to pay the bills, we would always have to rob Peter to pay Paul, consequently we had the electricity, gas and water turned off on numerous occasions, if I had let Anne look after the finances, I know for sure it would never had happened.

Somehow we managed to just about keep our heads above water, it was now 1969, Frank Lockyer had bought a big bungalow just up the road, I would do jobs for him most weekends, I remember on one occasion, he asked me if I was going to watch Neil Armstrong land on the Moon, I explained we never had a telly, what do you mean no telly, right lad get in that car, with that we raced off to Cranbrook, about four miles away, we stopped outside Banghams, to look in the window, they were the radio and TV specialist, come on he said, we went into the shop, he went straight up to the salesman and said I want the biggest and best TV you have in the shop, I want it delivered and working today, if you can't do that I will go somewhere else, they were all over him, and by teatime Anne and I had the best TV that money could buy, all up and running in our house. We enjoyed watching Neil Armstrong land on the Moon, and it was so nice to be able to come home from work, relax and watch the telly. That was Frank, if he liked you he would do anything for you, but if you ever let him down then God help you.

Bang hams. Not really changed much, still there today.

I continued to be busy, but unfortunately I got quinsy's, this is such an awful thing to get, I was in so much pain I had to be off work for quite a while, and what made matters worse, just before I went ill I was encouraged to go self employed, which seemed like a good idea at the time, so all I could claim was statutory sickness benefit, somehow we managed to pull through, but the work started to slow down and sometimes I only had a couple of days a week, things were getting dire, bills were building up, we were a couple of months behind with the mortgage, we just couldn't see how we would get out of this predicament.

Chapter 8.
101 The Street Willesborough Ashford Kent.

I decided to write a letter to the Building Society, to explain our dilemma, in those days they didn't mess about with all the letter writing, they came and visited, when he arrived he suggested we put the house up for sale, that way we will be able to pay them back and hopefully have a bit left for ourselves, it turned out to be the right thing to do at the time, after the house was sold and everything paid for, we ended up with something like two hundred and fifty pounds, which was a lot of money in those days.

During the course of the sale, I was approached by a builder friend of mine, he wanted to know if I was looking for work, I of course said yes, why not? it was thin on the ground with Tenterden and Cranbrook Plasterers, he put me in touch with Gwen, a Lady from Ashford, she did up properties to rent out, and was looking for a Plasterer, I got in touch and found myself in work almost straight away, I explained it toT&C Plasterers, they were fine about it so off I went.

This was the first time I had ever done a plastering job direct to the customer, and to be honest, I was very nervous, so I decided to charge so much a day, and get Gwen to supply the materials, it worked out well, she was happy I was happy, so all looked rosy. Gwen was an eccentric, the life and sole of the party one moment, and the Black Widow Spider the next, but I could live with that, as all her moods were directed at her young Boyfriend Michael, Gwen was about forty and Michael barely twenty. In many ways it was good fun watching then shout and scream at each other.

The house sale was completed, so we needed to find somewhere to live, of course! why didn't I think about it sooner, Gwen Landlady extraordinaire may have a property available, I asked her the question and we were in luck, she had this lovely old semi detached two bed roomed cottage, in Willesborough, which is Folkestone side of Ashford, it had just became vacant, it was seventeenth century, low beamed ceilings, inglenook fireplace, so different to our house at Biddenden, it was up a quiet road, with a triangular green opposite, which even had some swings for the kids, just the job.

We had great difficulty fitting our furniture into such a small place, but somehow we managed to get it all in, it didn't seem to matter, we felt at home the moment we walked through the door, and within a short space of time Anne had it all ship shape and Bristol fashion, do you know it was as if we had been there for years. Our neighbours were lovely, they were Mrs Varrier and her Daughter Francis, Mrs Varrier was well into her eighties and Francis was about sixty, we got on with them so well, Francis would baby sit for us now and again, Tina and Julia would stay at there's, and sleep in Francis's bed whilst she slept on the settee, once a week they even gave them pocket money, so yes we all felt really happy there, except for our cat Lucy, for whatever reason she would never come into the house, we tried to coax her, but she just wouldn't have it, if you tried to carry her in she would claw you to pieces, we reckoned it was haunted, or rather I reckoned it was haunted, I did experience some very strange things in that house, for instance, on a very regular basis, and at the time, I could almost say to the day when it would happen, if I recall it was about once a month, and no I wasn't drunk, I was always sober as a Judge. But first I will give you an idea of the layout of upstairs so it's easier to picture.

Access to the bedrooms were through a door in the lounge, the stairs very steep, would wind its way to our bedroom, which was of good size, with a big open fireplace next to the open staircase, which was brought back to bare brick, the breast itself covered most of the wall, we used to put our nick knacks in the little alcoves, and ledges. To get to Tina and Julia's bedroom you had to go through our bedroom, initially it was only a one bedroom cottage, but somewhere along the line they had installed a dormer window to the rear, which was glass the entire width of the cottage, it did make a good sized second bedroom, giving plenty of light in the winter it was bloody freezing, no radiators or double glazing in those days, very often the ice had to be scrapped off the inside, God knows how they got planning permission for that. Our bedroom floor sloped from one side to the other, we had to block the foot of our bed up it was that bad, it had a tiny leadlight window that looked out to the road, it was very cosy

Now back to the subject in hand, my experiences were always when I had just got into bed, , I never went to bed without leaving the light on, I was very uneasy about these things going on, and it only happened if I went to bed first. I would see either, a Lady, dressed like Florence Nightingale, or a Man, in a Sir Walter Rayleigh type of dress, never were they there together, but both would stand at the top of the stairs, and both would be just standing there smiling, although they never seemed to be a threat, I can tell you I would be trashing myself, this went on all the time we were living there, Tina also experienced goings on, she quite often would say, she could hear a baby crying next door, we know for a fact they never had a baby in that house, and the day we moved, Tina was crying, saying they don't want me to go, very strange.

I seemed to keep busy with the odd bit of work Gwen gave me, dribs and drabs started to come in from a little advert I put in the local rag. I also hand wrote, what seemed like hundreds of letters, that I distributed to all the local builders, and eventually it paid off, It netted me some very lucrative work, and in the main I was going to have a good relationship with them for several years to come. By now David had gone and got himself married to a girl called Elsie, they met in London and got wed at the Wandsworth Town Hall in 1968; David at that time was working for a tyre company, he got the sack for some reason or another and decided he wanted to move back to Kent, he wondered if Gwen had any properties to rent, as it happened, the place I help to do up for her was available, so David and Elsie came down to meet Gwen, she agreed to rent it to them, they were down there within the week. David and Elsie's house was only a short distance away, in Church Street South Willesborough, about two miles, which worked out to be quite useful.

Moving from London meant that both David and Elsie were without jobs, I think Elsie soon found a job in the local nut and bolt factory.

It was 1970, before too long, the plastering just got better and better, work was pouring in, David came on board. We called ourselves Shortle Bros, we were working quite often seven days a week, this went on for some time, and it was getting more and more difficult to get through the work, load so we decided if we had any chance of keeping everyone happy and hopefully expanding the business we needed more help.

What we really wanted was someone we knew, and was good on the tools, I suggested Derek Gurr, and he hadn't long left. T&C Plasterers, I knew he was long distance lorry driving, being married I think he was keen to get a job that would not keep him away from home. So I suggested to David that I go and see him, and offer him a job, we both agreed, off I trot to Cranbrook to see Derek, the first meeting was a bit awkward, as he ended up marrying Ann from Southborough, she was the girl if you recall I was going out with before I started going out with the other Anne. And this was the first time I have seen her since the day I told her I had found someone else, there was nothing to worry about, she was fine and our chat went well, Derek was keen to come on board, so all he had to do was to hand in his notice.

Over the next few years Shortle Bros did well, and within four years we had up to ten plasterers working for us, Derek stayed with us for a couple of years or so, he actually moved to Ashford and bought a house during his stay with us, he became a self employed taxis driver, I think he is still doing that to this day, I believe he moved a few years ago to somewhere like Bournmouth, I didn't really keep in touch after he left, we got on well, but I suppose it is fair to say not big buddies.

Rick posing whilst on a break from plasterering in front of the Lantern Hotel and Restaurant. Charing near Ashford Kent.

One very special Employee of ours was a guy called Fred Gore, I was advertising for plasterers, and Fred phoned up, I asked him to pop round to see me, I remember to this day seeing Fred walking up my garden path wearing a cheese cutter, he looked so old, and so thin, in fact he was sixty six, he knocked on the door, our back door was only about five foot six inches high, Fred was well over six foot, I asked Fred to come in, he had to bend right over to get through the door, as he crouched down to get through, the guttering that ran above the door whipped his cheese cutter off, he had to retrieve it from Lucy the cat's water bowel, Fred came in and sat on an upright chair with his cheese cutter placed covering his knee, which became a trade mark of his. I was very impressed with Fred and gave him an immediate start, he was from the old school, and although I was just a Lad to him, he always treated me with respect, as I to him, Fred lived in a tiny little bungalow, at Edgerton Forstal, nr Pluckley with his wife Esmie and Son Philip, Esmie was quite a bit younger than Fred, they got on well, we would quite often go and visit Fred and his family at weekends, and over the Christmas hols, it amazed us how she managed to cope in such a tiny place, typical old fashioned mum, always had a piny on, always had the kettle on and did a spread fit for a King. Fred worked for us for a number of years and in that time I can honestly say, he was without doubt the best person we ever had working for us, more of Fred later.

Just down the road from us was the Blacksmith arms Pub, we got to hear that they were looking for a cleaner, Tina and Julia were now both at primary school, so Anne applied for the job, which she got it, she was allowed to take the girls to work with her on school holidays, the Landlord Mr Bert Butcher, was soon nicknamed Burp Butcher, by the kids, because of all the burping he did, he was about seventy then, but pretty agile, he looked like the old type of Royal Air Officer, very smart with a small mastouche which was trimmed to perfection, he was a bit of a Ladies Man, always had that twinkle in his eye, a bit of a joker. In the man's loo would be a brass model of a young woman, with the words just below her skirt saying lift, if anyone lifted it, which was quite often, it would ring a bell in the bar, he was up to the same trick in the Ladies, but this time it was a Man in a Kilt. Bert got many hours of fun Chuckling to himself as the guilty party returned from either loo, but not knowing that Burp Butcher knew, and it was surprising the type of person that had a peek.

Mr Butcher was very strict on dress code, I didn't realise it, until one hot summers day, I fancied a pint so off I trot, in my shorts and t shirt, it was mid week, early evening, as I walked up to the bar, he told me to go home and get properly dressed, as he wouldn't serve me looking like that, the miserable old sod, he upset quite a few, and in the process lost quite a few customers, but he wasn't bothered, he ran the Pub how he felt it should be run, and bugger anyone else, His wife Mrs Butcher was a lovely Lady, she made the most exquisite sausage rolls that she sold in the pub, they were the dogs down bellows. Yes I know we are going to be very happy at 101 The Street Willesborough.

Anne with our two girls, Tina on left and Julia on the right when we were on holiday

Chapter 9.
My introduction to Grass Track and Speedway

I was in the Blacksmith Arms one day, I got talking to a chap that I vaguely new, his name was Tony, he brought up the subject of grass track racing, apparently something that was very popular in that area, he went on to explain what it was all about, bikes and side cars, which would race against each other, not together, bikes against bikes, sidecars against sidecars, on an grass oval track, that was hired from the local Farmer, the races were organised by a proper club, and were run throughout the season, at the end would be a champion for each class, I think from about 125cc up to a 1000cc. Tony invited me along to watch an event a couple of weeks later, I went along to a meeting at Romney Marsh, my first thought was, they were all bloody crackers, flying around on an oval circuit, flat out, sideways most of the time, to me they looked completely out of control, and all on a death wish. But the more I watched the more I could see that there was definitely a technique to it all, I went along to a few more meetings, getting to know some of the riders, in those days it was riders such as Roland Duke, Malcolm Simmons, he did speedway as well, the Banks Brothers Graham and Trevor, sadly Graham got killed at a meeting a few years later, now and again veteran Reg Luckhurst would make an appearance, on the Sidecars

was the only pair worth mentioning and they were the Penfold Brothers. Little did I know but this was to be my introduction to Racing.

I became very friendly with Tony, and before too long we were discussing what it would be like to have a go ourselves. We decided to buy a second hand bike, it would probably be a good idea if we start off with a low powered bike, just to see how we got on, we ended up with a 250cc BSA. It was in good condition, mind you we didn't have a clue what to do if anything went wrong.

We had the grass track bike, but never considered that we would have to find somewhere to ride it, to start with we used to take it on the Ashford Rugby field, which was at Kennington, went there a few times, before too long I was sliding the bike, which I thought was great, Tony was going around when the front locked up and threw him over the handle bars, he hurt himself, but not that much, so we packed up and went home, he called me the next day, to tell me that he didn't want to continue and felt we should put the bike up for sale, I was dead against this, and no way was I going to give up, so I told him that I would like to part exchange it for a bigger, more powerful machine, and what I get part exchange for the BSA I will give him his half, he said ok, I think he was upset that I wanted to continue, the problem with me is, if I find that I really want to do something, I will put everything into it, and it will take over my life I'm a bit obsessive.

I never had a clue what to do, I had a 250cc BSA that I didn't want, so I decided to buy the Motor Cycle News, and have a look through, to see if I could get any ideas what to do, lucky for me there was an article on a recent grass track meeting, and along with the write up was a section about bike suppliers etc, also an advertisement from the organising club, so I gave the club a call and explained my predicament, they were very helpful. They gave me a few helpful numbers including the name of a company that builds grass track bikes, it was Palmers of Maidstone. I went along to see them and as I arrived I felt completely out of my depth, there were all sorts of riders talking to each other, even the side car Aces the Penfold Brothers were there, I felt their eyes burning on the back of my neck, but luckily I do have that ability not show how nervous I was, anyway, as usual there was sod all to worry about, it was just me putting them all on pedestals, I soon got to find out that the grass track fraternity are a bunch of really good people, and will go out of their way to help each other.

I introduced myself to Mr Palmer, we had a long chat, he agreed to take the BSA in part exchange for a brand new 500cc JAP. Palmer Grass Track Bike. This had to be build and the build time was about six weeks, which was fine, the grass track season was about to finish, it would give me time to get the money together and hopefully find somewhere to practice.

Now Fred Gore lived well into the country, so I asked him if he knew any nice farmers that might let me ride my bike on one of his fields, Fred said he knew of one and that he will go and see him on Saturday, come Monday, Fred said he had been to see the Farmer who had no objection to letting me race around his field, he loves his whiskey, so keep him topped up with that, and you should be ok, I was over the moon, when the bike was ready, I was in that field going round and round, getting used to riding this 500cc, brand new bike, for a while I was frightened to damage it, but just like my first push bike that soon went out of the window.

My mind was now focussed on the grass track racing, I did everything possible to learn as much as I could, about how to get into the sport, I got back in touch with the guy that ran the club, he sent me the forms to get my licence, and enter the races. We were about a month away from the first race of the year; it was at Warehorn, near Hamstreet, which was just twenty minutes away. My first grass track meeting arrived in a flash, and all the planning and practice on the Farmers field were a thing of the past. Anne, Tina, Julia and my friend Tony came along, and to be fair he was brilliant, I think he was much better at helping than competing, there were thirty bikes in my first race I came twentieth, I was quite pleased with that, at least it wasn't last, the next race I was in twelfth place but came off, we watched the rest of the races, then packed up and went home, stopping for a beer in the Blacksmiths arms, all in all it was successful day, the weather was great, all us competitors were parked together around the perimeter of the track, it was a family outing for almost everyone, the competitor next to us was having a BBQ, they very kindly invited us to join them, Anne and the girls enjoyed the whole day. I was looking forward to the next race.

Although I was still busy plastering, it is the type of skill that once you master it, you don't even have to think about what you are doing, lots of people say it's amazing to watch someone plaster, and that it looks very therapeutic, so what I'm trying to say is, it gave me all the time in the world to think about my new goal in life, to plan, to think about the next race etc.

On our way to the meetings we would always stop at the ABC Stores, which was in Hythe Road Ashford, it had just been taken over by a Brian and Celia Ellma, I would have my car parked outside his shop, my bike would be hanging on a special made bike rack at the back of the car, Brian was like Marmite he either liked you or hated you, lucky for me he liked me, he showed interest in the fact that I did a bit of grass track racing, I often popped into ABC on the way home for a chat.

We got on extremely well, we even went on holiday together, it was then when he told me about his love for speedway.

On holiday with Brian. Brian and myself, seen here being very silly

The team he followed, was the Bell Vue Aces, speedway is very similar to grass track, but this time you would race on oval made of coarse packed sand, but called a cinder track, the perimeter was either boarded to about four feet high or had a meshed fence, Oh! and the bikes didn't have any brakes, they had a 500cc Jawa engine, ran on wood alcohol known as methanol, the engine was lubricated with Castrol R, which smelt fantastic, I even put it in my lawn mower because I loved the smell so much, a speedway bike was a total loss system, the frame of the bike would be filled with oil and as it circulated through the engine, it would then drip out of the sump onto the track, the idea being the oil was perfect every time. Brian asked me if I fancied having a go at speedway, I really didn't know what to say, I said let me think about it, he suggested we went to our local speedway track, and have a look, which was at Canterbury, they were known as the Canterbury Crusaders, I have never been to a speedway meeting, the Crusaders would have a home meeting every other Saturday evening, so off we went, it was early in the season, by the time the meeting was due to start the flood lights came on, the atmosphere was fantastic, and compared with grass track racing, it looked so professional, the teams would do a slow lap of the track, whilst being presented by the commentator, it looked so colourful, the fans were all around the perimeter of the boarded track, with their programmes, scarves, rattles and wearing a t shirt and hat of their favourite rider. The main riders then were Barney Kennet (Captain) Jaffer the gaffer Purkis, Graham Clifton, and Reg Luckhurst. I was looking forward to this, but wondered why everyone stood so far back from the track, being a new boy I thought great, let's get a good view, I was standing against the boards, the four riders two from each team were on the grid, each with a different coloured cover on their helmets to show their grid position, the tapes went down and off they went, apparently these bike accelerate from nought to sixty in two point four seconds, well before the first corner they were all sliding inches from each other, the rear wheel seemed to be almost past the front, wow what a spectacular site, out of the first corner down the back straight, which took no time at all. Then sideways again as they enter the final corner, I was situated at the exit and soon to find out why the crowd were well back, as they exited, I was completely covered in shale, and what an idiot I felt, goes without saying I would never be that close again.

I must admit I was hooked, although I did think they were all bloody mad, Brian could tell I was excited, and he knew I would give him the right answer, I still said I will think about it, which wasn't long, in fact I said yes before we got home, he was delighted, he said if I was serious he would sponsor me, and purchase the first Speedway bike, everything seemed to be moving at one hundred miles an hour, after all, I had barely started, just a few grass track races, with just one win under my belt, riding speedway did intrigued me, I couldn't wait to get the ball rolling.

Anne was happy for me, but at the same time concerned, it was and still is a very dangerous sport, she knew I was serious, and was aware that I wouldn't give up lightly. I now had to find the best way to get into this highly dangerous sport, fortunate for me Reg Luckhurst lived just down the road, in Great Chart; he had a small holding, and a business that built and repaired speedway bikes. I decided to go and see him, he didn't know me from Adam, I told him what I was after, and again just like the Guy that gave me advise on Grass Tracking, he was very forth coming, he advised me to purchase a good second hand bike, then go round the country, visit as many tracks as possible, book myself in to practice and training sessions to see how I get on. This all made good sense, Reg had a good second hand Jawa for sale, (Jawa engined bikes where the ones in those days), so I hot footed back to Brian, at ABC Stores to give him the news, he agreed with everything

Reg said, including the cost of the bike, we went along the following day to see him, Brian had a long chat with Reg, gave him a deposit on the bike and made arrangements to collect it in a couple of weeks time. The excitement was killing me, I have a bike, the only problem now is can I do it justice?

There was no stopping Brian, he got in touch with all the tracks that do practice and tuition, the favourite choice was Mildenhall, it was a mile or two past the American Air force Base, stuck out in the middle of nowhere, the track was quite small, but a good choice for a beginner, at that time Mildenhall were in the premier division, the facilities were very good, they had a club house and bar, the staff were friendly and always gave help and advice, we would go there on a weekly basis. In those days it wasn't just a trip up the motorway. From Ashford it seemed to take for ever to get there. Before too long I was riding with confidence, the practice sessions were always run as races, so it immediately gave you an idea, of what it was all about, even if I say so myself I was starting to look like a speedway rider, my first big crash was here, I dropped the bike at the start, the bike flew into the fence, I was left on the track in quite a bit of pain, my knee had become dislodged, it was sticking out a a ridiculous angle, without thinking, I pushed it back into place, my bike was less fortunate, that was the end of our practise for today, we had to get new front forks, and a new wheel from Reg Luckhurst, he was delighted that I had come off, because he said at least I was pushing myself, passed my own capabilities, and not to worry as that is the way forward,

I suppose he was correct, or maybe just sadistic. We were soon back at Mildenhall, the team Manager had a word with Brian, he suggested I sign up for the Reading Racers speedway training school, they are looking for juniors to sign for their club, he felt I was a good candidate, and should consider going.

Brian would always come with me, I was treated like a pro, he would drive to and from the circuit, as far as I can recall, he even paid for the petrol, he must have been able to afford it, and on top of that, he was in his element, probably a dream come true for him, his own speedway rider.

Brian was soon on the phone to Reading Racers, apparently the Team Manager of Mildenhall had mentioned my name to them, so they were keen that I attended. The course was to be run by the three top riders of Reading Racers, Dave Jessup, Bernie Leigh and John Davis, at that time they were one of the best teams in the country, and all those mentioned rode for England in the world Cup, so they knew what they were talking about.

The three day course was to be run in the closed season, the top three pupils would be signed up and put in the second half races, with a view, if they were any good enough, farmed out to a lower divisions, to race properly in a team, such as Canterbury Crusaders.

The day soon arrived, we made our way to Reading, as always we arrived far too early, Brian was like that, and so am I really, it was a nervous time, we all met in the club house, all thirty two of us, we were ask to sign the indemnities, Dave Jessup opened the meeting by introducing everybody to everybody else, which was a good way to break the ice, I felt I was the most nervous, but I'm sure we all felt the same. Dave introduced us to Bernie Leigh and John Davis, he told us about their achievements, I think Bernie then took over with a classroom session, we then had a cuppa, prior to venturing out to the pits, and allocated a bay just like the teams do, then instructed to warm our bikes up, to start the engine you would put the back wheel on a stand to raise it off the ground, then spin the back wheel round until it burst into life, once warmed up we were told to cut the engines, at that point they did an inspection of the bikes, just to make sure everything was safe and working properly, if anything was wrong or needed attention we were told either to put it right or given advise on what needed to be carried out. I was wearing my new leathers that Brian had given me, they were yellow and green, not my favourite colour, but Brian came from Norwich and supported Norwich Football Club, so yellow and green it was.

We made our way out onto the track, four at a time, we were told to keep a good distance from each other, get used to the track and do nothing silly, it was my turn and the feeling of riding round a division one track was amazing, we had tuition all the time, pulling us in if they thought our technique wasn't quite right, the day ended with some races, nobody came a cropper, and by the end of the day we had all got to know each other and went away happy looking forward to day two. I fell asleep in the car, leaving Brian to drive all that way without any conversation, but he was cool, and buzzing just like me. I expect he was day dreaming all sorts of daft things.

Day two of the Reading Racers Speedway Training School, the atmosphere was so much better than day one, there was an excitement about the place, I was still nervous, but I think it was a different sort of nervousness, this time it was all about doing well and hopefully showing Dave Jessup and Co, I was a contender. It certainly wasn't the best of days, it was raining, the track had been graded which means they pull a large rake behind a tractor to loosen the surface of the track, this will give it more grip, and when the track is wet, for some reason it has even more grip, the morning went well, there was a series of races I think we had about four each, I was first in two, second in one and third in another, which was a good as anyone else, so I went to lunch feeling quite strong.

After lunch the heavens opened up, in some places there was standing water, some of the Lads decided to sit it out, but I thought this is my chance to show I'm a gritty bugger, I won my first two races, by now the weather really was nasty, I decided to go out one more time, I was leading quite easily, but as I exited the final bend to come onto the home straight, my bike found too much grip, it lifted the front wheel off the ground, and I ended up in the fence, I was still hanging on to the handle bars, as they hit the fence, it snatched my shoulder and broke my collar bone, and big toe, Dave Jessup rushed over to see if I was ok, apart from the pain I was fine, obviously we had to go to the hospital, so they allowed us to leave our bike at the track, and go to Reading General, we were in there ages, they put me in something called a collar and cuff and that was it, just out of Reading we stopped for a cuppa in a Little Chef, I called Anne but never told her what had happened, as I didn't want to worry her, the pain was quite bad during our journey home, and I was pissed off because I thought I had blown my chances, Dave Jessup left a message at Brians shop, to say if we could make it tomorrow he would be grateful, although I was still in pain, I decided to go, to be a spectator, and congratulate the winner, plus see who has been signed up with Reading Racers, even though I thought it wouldn't be me. Dave, Bernie and John all popped over to see me the moment we arrived. The day seemed to drag and drag, mainly because I couldn't get comfortable, thankfully the last day finished early, all that was left to do, was go to the Club House for a de-brief and awards. Dave Jessup gave the de-brief, he summarised by mentioning almost everybody, with the usual how well everyone had done, then onto the awards, he basically said that we are so pleased that Rick Shortle could make it today, if he had been able to ride, we all felt he may well have won the award, which shocked me, but gave me so much confidence to carry on, a chap named Ian Gledhill won, sadly a couple of years later he had a nasty accident whilst riding, and ended up paralysed from the waist down, I was awarded second which meant I would be a junior rider for a Division one Team, Reading Racers, Fan- bloody- tastic, Brian was in tears, I was in shock, gone was the pain, well for a minute or so, we couldn't wait to let Celia and Anne know the good news.

On the way home we were so happy, we began talking about the future, I said, we need the latest bike, the one to have is the Godden frame with the new engine to speedway, the Westlake. Brian, I know would not be able to fund this on his own, so we agreed to pay half each, I went along to Don Godden's factory in West Malling, he explained everything, including the cost, which was an awful lot of money, but if you want to do well, you have to have the right equipment, and the Godden Westlake was the one to have. I placed an order for an all silver machine, placed my deposit, and decided to pay so much a week, estimated time of build was three months, I was sure it would be paid for by then. The Plastering business was doing well, so we didn't have to worry too much. By now my whole life was around the racing, I couldn't think of anything else, that's where the obsession comes in.

The big day had arrived, the day I collect my new Godden Westlake, I remember arriving at Godden's factory, it was all ready for me, Don wasn't around but his main Man was, Graham Hurry, Graham was one of Europe's top Long track riders, even he was excited, nobody had chosen a bike in the colour of silver before, and with the little touches of black guards and chequered seat etc it looked fabulous, he went through it in every detail, and when he fired it up, it sounded completely different to my second hand Jawa. They took a photo of Graham handing it over, which was put on their reception wall. I loaded it onto the back of my car and speedily drove off to show Brian and Celia, they thought it was fantastic, all I had to do, was exactly the same as I had to do with the Jawa, prove I could do it justice

My Godden Westlake Speedway Bike.

We booked ourselves into several practice sessions; Wimbledon Don's track in London, Kings Lynn, Reading, Hackney, Iwade, and Eastbourne, to give me experience of as many tracks as possible, before the season began. I was looking forward to my first meeting at Reading, it was surreal arriving at the circuit as a proper signed up driver, even though I was only a junior, second half driver, my first race was against all the other juniors, I finished second, my next race was against Bernie Leigh, Peter Collins and another rider from Belleview, all top riders, unbelievably I made the gate and was leading into the first corner, I was leading for two laps, only to overcook it and slide gently off, I remounted but obviously ended up last, I was far from disappointed, having lead three of England's top racers, this result did me no harm whatsoever, Brian had a telephone call from Reading Racers, to say I had been farmed out to Canterbury Crusaders, my local circuit, where it all started, hanging over the boards getting covered in shale, at that moment it seems like a fairy tale

Chapter 10.
It all goes wrong.

We decided to set out a programme of serious testing, at as many tracks as we could, I was on fire, and quietly knew if I did the practice, I would hopefully deliver the goods. My new Godden Westlake was the match of anything, and it soon became obvious that I could mix it with the best, no matter what circuit we went to, I was competitive, that was until we decided to go to the Hackney Hawks track in London, it was a dry Saturday afternoon, we unloaded the bike, got it set up and ready to go, I went to the changing rooms to get into my leathers, when a chap came and approached me, he was selling accident insurance, he assured me, if I signed on the dotted line, there and then, and had an accident racing today, I would be covered for loss of earnings, HP on the car and mortgage or rent etc. As we had just moved from our beloved 101 The Street and bought ourselves a detached house, just down the road, I thought why not, it could always be cancelled, so I signed up, and made my way to the pits, Brian was warming the bike up, I was ready to go, I have never been to Hackney before, it's a lovely track and I was looking forward to riding it, as usual we were sent out in fours, doing four lap races, I was doing well, the bike was perfect, it was flying, every time I went out, my pace was good enough to be up there, this continued well into the afternoon, I think it was probably my final race, I gated well, and was leading, on the second lap going into turn three, my Westlake lifted its front wheel, I tried to get it down without success, Hackney's fence is wire mesh, I got ever closer to the fence, and I knew I would hit it, I slammed into the fence, my right leg was caught between the engine and the fence, I can't remember to much, apart from being thrown over the fence into the Dog track. I can remember everything going dead quiet, I wasn't in pain, I suppose it was the adrenaline pumping in, then all of a sudden the pain came in, there were people everywhere, the first aiders were there, just comforting me, saying they were waiting for the paramedics to arrive from Hackney Hospital, they were there within minutes, with a stretcher which was laid by my side, they then cut my leathers to inspect my leg, I couldn't quite hear what they were saying, but I had a notion it was serious, I do remember them strapping my legs together, and I recall saying they have it too tight and there is a knot in the rope, they said something to each other like, that's no knot he can feel, it's the bone poking out of his leg, by this time I was on gas and air, being taken to the Ambulance and whisked off to Hackney General, taking gas and air all the way, I can't remember anything from the time I was wheeled into the Hospital until the next day. The morning arrived and I found myself in plaster from the tip of my toe, right up to my groin, with a window in the plaster half way down my shin bone, I was told it was for the surgeon to keep an eye on the leg, because of the shale, they were concerned about infection, it was a very bad break, I had lost some two inches of bone, so the surgeon put a pin through my heel and stretched the leg until the plaster set, with hope the bone would grow, and my leg would remain the correct length, I had a few operations, one was to stretch the leg yet again, I remember coming round, after a trip to theatre, I couldn't move, I was terrified, thinking I was paralysed. I heard later they had given me an injection in the groin to relax me, but it went all wrong, it was almost a day before I could move, and what a relief when I could, all sorts of things were going through my mind. I have to say although Hackney Hospital was a bit of a dump, the nurses were fantastic, nothing was too much trouble, I even got them to nip out and get me burger and chips on a couple of occasions. I was in hospital about a month, a long time for a broken leg, I was desperate to be back at home, I kept bothering them to let me go, in the end they allowed me to go home, I said my goodbyes and left, although I was glad to leave, us patients seemed to get on well and have a bit of a laugh, you do see some funny things happen in Hospital, for example in the bed opposite, was an old Man that was suffering from bed sores, to help relieve this, the nurses would get him out of bed, and sit him on a chair that had a rubber ring, this allowed his bottom not to come in contact with anything, which must be lovely if you have bed sores. Now that's not funny, but the funny bit was, when he was put back into bed, he would fall asleep, and an old codger from a bed further down the ward, would trot up, go over to the rubber ring, lift up his clothes and pee in the ring, and although disgusting the rest of us were in fits, and every time it was about to happened, it went round the ward in sign language, so we were all ready to see the next performance, that in its self looked hilarious, with arms flaying, heads nodding, etc. And although I was sent home, I hadn't seen the last of Hackney General, there's a long way to go yet. Brian drove me home, he was marvellous, during my stay at Hackney General, he came to visit every day, he brought Anne along as well, it was a long haul for him every day from Ashford Kent.

The moment I got home, I realised the hospital were right, and I was wrong, they wanted me to stay in for a while longer, I soon found out, even the simplest things were so difficult to do at home, and for the first couple of days I even considered going back. Thankfully we got into a routine and found ways around any problems, I had to sleep down stairs for quite a while, and no way would I be able to manage the tight and twisty stairs, as time went by things got easier, the leg was less painful, and I was ready to venture out of the house, the plastering business was still very busy, during my stay in hospital, a good friend of ours that worked for the Prudential offered to help, which was invaluable, he would run round the jobs, to see if the men were ok or required material etc, Anne did the wages, so everything went without too many hiccups. Remember the Accident Insurance chap, well he came good, I was covered, which meant I would receive quite a nice income from them each month until I went back to work, result.

We hired a wheel chair from the Red Cross, which at first was no use, as I couldn't bent my leg, because the plaster cast was from my groin to the tip of my toe, I got David to knock up something, that would allow me to sit in the chair with my leg straight, it was a piece of wood that was about eight inches wide to rest my leg on, he put sides on it, to keep my leg safe, it then had a wider piece fixed to it which I sat on, hoping that the weight of my body would keep my leg suspended, this worked fine, until we went over a bump, which would make the whole contraption bounce up and down, on a few occasions the bloody contraption would slip forward under the weight, and the chair would land tits up on the floor, however it proved to have more going for it than against.

On my road to recovery, in the garden with Julia our youngest. They were the crutches the little rascals would adjust.

During my time in plaster, I did experience some funny moments, for example, Tina and Julia were little buggers, I had telescopic crutches that could be adjusted, to suit the size of the patient, quite easy to change, once the girls discovered how, they would quietly slide the crutches down to the shortest length, when I got up to use them, on more than one occasion I would end up on the grass, because by the time the crutch had reached the floor I was already on my way over, the little darlings.

A couple of not so funny experiences, when I was out and about, I would get Fred Gore to take me round to check out the jobs, he had a Ford Cortina, which was ideal, a I could sit in the back, with my leg placed between the front seats, on one occasion we were driving down a narrow lane near Rhodes Minnis, as we went around a bend, there was a horse gently jogging along with its rider, Fred was getting impatient, he then did something that I would never expect Fred to do, he blasted his horn, the horse reared up, almost dismounted the rider, Fred jammed his brakes on, throwing me forward, and all Fred said was bloody horses, shouldn't be on the road.

On another occasion Fred was driving me back from Charing, as you come out of Charing there is a bit of a duel carriageway by the Crematorium, it was pouring with rain, we were in the fast lane, when Fred's windscreen wipers packed up, he casually stopped, to see if he could sort them out, there I was sitting in the back, leg between the front seats, cars flashing by, horns going off, whilst Fred was leaning over the front of his car trying to fix the bloody wipers, I was positively pooing myself, good old Fred. Both incidents were terrifying at the time, but now they are so funny. Needless to say I never used him to run me about again. It was back to my Man from the Pru.

I had to visit Hackney General on numerous occasions, after a couple of months the plaster was taken off to see how things were progressing, unfortunately due to the loss of bone it wasn't knitting together, during the next eighteen months the plaster was removed and the leg inspected, god knows how many times, after all this, the surgeon advised me the mending process was too slow, and the only course of action was to have a bone graft, this meant going back in hospital to have some bone taken from my hip, to put in my leg, which would do the trick. I was back in Hackney General within a couple of weeks, operation proved a success, and within four months I was out of plaster for good. I was in plaster for almost two years which is one hell of a long time by anyone's standards, and Boy was I glad to hear the news, imagine your leg being encased in plaster for that amount of time, when it finally showed the true light of day it didn't look like a leg, it had lost all its muscle, and was covered in thick scaly skin, the knee joint had ceased up, and unfortunately, even though they tried to stretch it, to get it back to its former length, my leg was still over an inch short, something I have to live with, which was miniscule compared what I had been through. The most important thing was, I had my leg back, and soon I would be walking properly again.

Hackney referred me to my local Hospital in Ashford for physiotherapy, I was now on the road to full recovery, and it was explained by the physiotherapist, that it would be up to me how long it would take to get back normal, it was going to be a long painful journey.

Chapter 11.
My road to recovery.

I arrived home early afternoon, and what I did next was ridiculous, just before my accident, I purchased a new car, this has sat outside the front of my house all that time, I decided in my stupidity to try and drive it, I remember hobbling up and down the front garden trying to get some sort of movement in my knee, which was next to nothing, but undeterred, I work out a way to drive, basically I would use one of the crutches to operate the throttle and my left leg to brake, I remember to this day, driving up the road at a snail's pace, it was a nightmare, but I did it, Anne went bloody berserk, which was understandable, I promised not to drive again until I was passed fit enough to do so.

I attended physic twice a week, the treatment included bending the knee or trying to, I was advised to get myself a bike, have the saddle as high as it would go, so the leg only bent slightly, once I could bend the leg without a problem, I should lower the saddle bit by bit, being impatient I try to lower the saddle too soon, this was extremely painful, but it did the job, I also had to stand in front of a mirror and practice walking, my injured leg tended to turn out and looked awful, I can understand now what the physic meant, when she said it was up to me, you just have to push yourself, and it's surprising when you are at physiotherapy, how many patients are just too scared to go through the pain barrier, within a few weeks I was signed off, they gave me exercises to do, they felt I would be ok to do the rest myself.

I continued to exercise by walking, not running, unfortunately I can't run even to this day, I did a lot of bike riding, and swimming. My leg was feeling much better, and although it wasn't a pretty sight, due to the loss of flesh, it is now stronger than the other one, but I hate having to jump off anything, which I'm sure is psychological.

With the healing processing going well, I was getting itchy feet, and again I decide to do something quite ridiculous, I borrowed a speedway bike, booked myself into Ollie Nigrens International Speedway School, at Kings Lynn. I had to prove to myself, that I could still do it, Anne was upset, and couldn't understand or believe I wanted to do such a thing, why after all I've been through, how on earth could I even considering it. My mind was made up, so off I went, with Brian to Kings Lynn. I must admit to being very nervous, the super confident Rick wasn't there, we arrived, Ollie gave us a briefing, I jumped on my bike, slid it through the first corner, and continued to do several laps, which were not far off from being competitive, I came into the pits, Brian looked delighted, but not for long, I got off my bike, and told him that I have done what I wanted to do, and that I have no intention of going back to speedway, that was the last time I ever sat on a speedway bike, I knew in my heart the accident had taken away that little extra bit I would need to do well.

Brian was devastated, he did all he could on the way home to get me to change my mind, and nothing he said would do that, it was a great shame but the right decision. Sadly the end of something I was good at, and who knows how good I may have been, we will never know.

I got home and told Anne the news, which I knew would please her no end, Anne is one in a million, and she would never stop me from doing anything, I am a really fortunate person to have such a caring loving wife, something I took for granted, and to be honest it was something I tended to do throughout my racing career.

Chapter 12.
What's next?

I decided to put it all behind me, and concentrate on getting fit, as I was far from that, although I had got back on a bike, I still had difficulty in walking properly, and no way, apart from visiting the jobs was I ready to go back full time, it was fortunate for me, I had several plasterers, bringing in money, otherwise it would have been a different kettle of fish.

I spent most of my time at home recuperating, but me being me, I soon got bored, I was sick and tired of reading the newspaper, and doing the crossword, they get so repetitive, after a while I could do them in no time at all, I was reading a magazine one day, there was a feature on the Motor Racing Stables at Brands Hatch, that were offering a 10% discount on the initial course, in those days they actually gave proper race instruction, nothing like it is today. Nowadays, you just get an experience on driving a single seater racing car, or saloon car, around a circuit, followed by some young hot shoe showing off, when he or she drives you around as fast as they can, telling you it's only about 70%. Don't have any of it; they are driving to their limit and sometimes beyond it.

I decided to book myself into the initial course, which was a few weeks later, I told Anne but cannot remember her comments, initially I just needed to do something, and although it wasn't a bike, it was driving around a track, and to me after speedway, what was there to worry about?

I arrived at Brands Hatch, the last time I went there, was with Mick Kennet on his Triumph Bonneville, to watch a bike race, years ago, It was a horrible wet day, which brought back memories of being at the Reading Racers Training School, this made me a little nervous, in those days at Brands you had to sign on in a building next to the Kentagon restaurant, once signed on we were escorted over to the centre of the circuit, where the racing school was operated from, we climbed some steel stairs, then led into a viewing gallery situated above the main start finish line, it was great place to be, you could see the whole of the Indy circuit, apart from one small section, that's as the drivers climb the hill to druids and disappear under the trees, they reappear again as they exit the Druids Hairpin.

Motor Racing Stables was owned and run by the legendry Brian Jones, who is well known for his commentating skills, he is still commentating to this day, and without doubt, one of the best around, he has such a wealth of knowledge, he can put it across in such a easy understanding way, the spectators love him.

Our briefing Instructor was an older guy by the name of Les Ager; his briefing was brilliant, completely different to those we had at any Speedway track, he asked if anyone had done racing, I put my hand up and said that I had done a bit of speedway, he then said, I will expect you to be smooth, all bike racers are smooth, I wished I had kept my mouth shut, he went through everything in detail, explained the layout of the circuit, the flags, rev limit aloud at this initial stage etc. With the briefing over we were told to stay there until called, as I waited I watched the cars going round, trying to get an idea of what is expected, as far as I could tell, nothing is expected other than being smooth and sensible, so this is what I intended doing, at last my name was called, I made my way to the operating tower below, as I entered a couple of instructors were facing the circuit, timing cars as they went passed below, I was greeted by the Chief Instructor, it was the late great Tony Lanfranci, and what a character he was, Tony was someone I got to know extremely well, more of that later, he gave me a bit of a briefing, told me to find a helmet, then sent me down to the pit lane to meet my instructor, which happened to be Les Ager, so thoughts of being smooth flashed through my mind, Les asked me to get into the driver's seat, and make myself comfortable, he helped me belt up, then made his way round to the passenger seat, he again explained what we were about to do, which was, I would drive him for four laps, he would keep quiet, unless I was driving dangerously, we would then come into the pits, he would give me marks out of one hundred on a sheet provided, I had to get 60% to get through to the next stage, I drove out onto the track, Brands is nothing like it looks from the outside, it's so undulating, I was doing the best I could, trying to get the lines and braking correct, the four laps seem to take forever, finally I was back in the pit lane, we came to a halt just below the control tower, Les asked me if I had enjoyed it, I said something like I think so, but a bit nervous, he remarked that I had driven well, maybe a bit slow, but nothing to worry about at this stage, he gave me 85%, much more than I ever expected, Les then took the controls, and explained, that he will be taking me round for two laps to give me an idea of what it's all about, He slowly went out onto the circuit and did the first lap quite slow explaining the lines, the braking and gear changing places, as we exited clearways, Les put his foot down, and it was still raining, we flew over the start finish line, climbed up to Paddock Hill Bend, he turned into Paddock, which seemed frightenly too fast, he negotiated Paddock the car was sliding, but I could tell he was in full control, my knuckles went white, he continued at speed for the rest of the lap, at the time I thought there is no way I could ever drive a car like that, and the memory of my introduction to driving round a race circuit, will always be Les Ager flying into Paddock in the wet.

Les gave me my sheet and told me to report back to Tony in the Tower, I handed my sheet over, Tony had a look, and he gave me two options, either ten laps in the saloon car, which at that time was a Sunbeam Talbot or five laps in a single seater, which was a Formula Ford 1600cc. I opted for the saloon, I think mainly because it was raining, and also I had just driven one, so I was familiar with it, he gave me a limit of 4000 revs, which I thought very low, but believe me in the wet I had a job to reach that apart from the main straight, I completed my laps without any problems, I made my way into the pits, then up to see Tony, he gave me a bit of banter, handed me my score sheet, explained I was through to the next stage, and if I wanted to book it up, go to where I signed on, I must admit I was hooked, dear oh dear, here we go again, I went and booked up the next stage, little did I know the Lady that took the booking was a certain Desiree Wilson, the only Woman to get to formula One.

Although at this stage, doing what I was doing didn't mean I would become a racing driver, it never entered my head to be one, I just needed to do something, so at the moment, that's all it is, a bit of fun and enjoyment. I went home told Anne how I got on, and decided to play it down a bit.

My next session was the intermediate, which I sailed through, then came the advanced stage, at this stage, it's a 6000 rev limit, with a time set by an instructor in the same car, at the same rev limit, the Instructor to set a time, was ex Formula One driver Tony Trimmer, it's getting a bit serious now, my first run out was just outside his time, I knew I could do better, so I asked Tony Lanfranci if it was possible to do a further ten laps, he called the booking office and they said ok, I'm glad I booked in those extra laps because I got through, Tony said I had done a great job, he explained that the Motor Racing Stables operated a closed race meeting, once a month, and those that get through the advanced stage will be invited to race against each other, can he put my name forward, I said yes, the cost was £60 a meeting, which was cheap even in those days, he advised me to get down here as much as I could to do timed laps, the more I did the better I will be.

Up to now I hadn't said much to anybody, I knew David was more interested in cars than bikes, so I decided to tell him what I was up to, I invited him along to my next visit to Brands, it would be great to have your brother involved, we bought a stop watch, so he could time me, and compare it with the timing tower, they were never wrong, but it got David involved, we went to Brands as much I could afford, my lap times were good, and always within a tenth of a second of each other, which apparently is the sign of a good driver.

My actual race was only a week away, it was on a Wednesday, David came along, we could see that most of the other drivers had obviously been before, they were all clad in race suits and boots, with their own designer hats, I rolled up as usual in my lucky green and black rugby shirt, a pair of jeans, plimsolls and no hat, I would borrow a racing school one, I always wore this shirt, for some unknown reason I considered it to be lucky, and I told David I would not invest in a race suit until I won my first race.

The meeting began, I had two races, third in my first race, and my second race I won, fantastic, the awards took place in the Kentagon, I recall Brian Jones, doing his usual speech, remarking, that at this stage the Motor Racing Stables Pupils, not only begin to drive like Race

Drivers, but look like Race Divers as well, he then looked over to me, and said apart from Rick Shortle, it's nice to be different, I went up and received my cups for third and first. David smirked and said something like; you better get yourself a race suit now.

Recieving a trophy for my first win. Brands Hatch

I competed in eight Motor Racing Stables races, and apart from my first race I won every other one.

I was now beginning to feel comfortable in a race car; my confidence was a bit like I used to have, when racing my Godden Westlake. The bug has bit, I didn't want to continue entering the closed races, my sights were now set on trying to find a way to actually race at a proper race meeting, whilst I was trying to sort this out, Motor Racing Stables organised a race in the School cars, at a proper race meeting, at Brands, I was invited and obviously accepted, I went on to win, what a start and what a stroke of luck getting into a full blown race meeting without trying.

I didn't have a clue how to go about it, so I decided to have a chat with the BRSCC. They were based at Brands, the Guy there, asked me what I wanted to race, I didn't really know, although at the time Tony Lanfranci, was racing a Volkswagen Sirocco and winning everything, little did I realise at the time, you have to be a great driver like Tony, plus have a great Team around you to supply a car, good enough to win. I suggested saloons, but he said he knew how well I was doing at the school, and advised me to think about going into Formula Ford 1600cc. That is by far the best way to get recognised, so led by his advice I went home and had a word with David, he agreed, the next move was to find a car.

Chapter 13
1981 a lot to learn.

David and I decided to buy the Autosport and Motoring news, they are the Motor Racing bibles, and have everything you need to know, from race reports, to race cars for sale, to be honest we hadn't a clue what we were looking for, we obviously had a budget, and a tight one at that, and thought it would be a good idea, to get a slightly older, second hand one, to use as a learning curve, we scanned the mags and in the end chose an RP21 a winning car in its heyday.

We trotted off to have a look at the RP21. Again didn't have a clue what we were looking for, had to take the seller on face value, and hope he wasn't trying to pull the wool over our eyes, or have you trousers down as David would say, the car looked in good nick, so after a bit of bartering, we were the proud owners of a RP21 Formula Ford Racing Car.

My first Race Car. The RP21

My next step was to have another word with the BRSCC. To get advise on what is required to go racing, they said I would need a race licence, which would take a couple of weeks, and to join the BRSCC, the British Racing and Sports Car Club. They are one of several Clubs that organise the race meetings, I thought it would be a good idea to have a some general testing, prior to my debut, which requires a race licence, so we will have to wait until my licence arrives, I joined the BRSCC and booked in a couple of races at Brands Hatch, it's all happening, I applied for my licence and paid express application, which means I will get my licence in just a few days, my licence arrived within four days, so we were up and running, I phoned Brands, and booked in for general testing on the following Tuesday, we couldn't wait, but didn't know what to expect, neither was I prepared for such a baptism of fire, off to Brands Hatch we go, we arrived and unloaded the car, topped it up with fuel, checked the tyre pressures which was a guess, and were as ready as we would ever be, so pit lane here we come, there were quite a few cars there that day, so the Marshalls only allowed a certain a number of cars out at a time.

Although I had driven around this circuit quite a few times before, my first days testing was quite unnerving, in the race school I would drive the circuit in a very controlled manner, but now it was a free for all, the race cars were of all types, which meant some were far more powerful than my Formula Ford, I spent most of my first days testing just looking in the mirrors and keeping out of their way.

I knew David was a little bit disappointed, he expected me to be much quicker than I was, in fact I was as well, still at least we took the race car home in one piece, on the way home we chatted about our first real test day, and both agreed we had a bloody long way to go, compared with the other Formula Fords, I was way off the pace, undeterred I booked us into another test session the following week, and the week after etc, our times were getting better but not good enough, after a while we got to know a few drivers, and decided to ask for advice, on setting the car up, I remember talking to a chap named Trevor Styles, he was one of the front runners in the Champion of Brands series for Formula Fords, after explaining one or two things to him, he just said I've followed you round, and basically you're not going quick enough, and although that car will not win races, it will certainly do better lap times than that, I was devastated, I honestly thought I was driving my car to the limit, obviously not, with that

David said I better get my finger out or give up, one thing with David he will tell me how it is, and although I didn't like to hear it, he was right, giving up, was something I didn't want to do, before our next session the following week, I gave it some thought, and realised Trevor was right, I was driving around too much within myself, it was time to push past what I thought to be safe, and try to find my limits, I hadn't had a spin or gone off once, and thinking about it, even the good drivers were having mishaps now and then.

We had two more test sessions before my first race, I knew it was absolutely imperative to get out there and improve, I never said anything to David about my thoughts; I was hoping to surprise him. And surprise him I did, during our next session, I had improved my lap times dramatically, by the end of the test day I was within a couple of seconds a lap, off a reasonable time, which wasn't fantastic, but to us a major breakthrough, we went home that day, grinning from ear to ear, I had spun off a few times, damaging the car slightly, but feeling great, all we had to do now was to rush around and find bits, so we could repair the car in time for our final test session before the first race.

When we got home the postman had delivered the passes and details of the race meeting, including a programme, which I scurried through to look for my name, and there it was, Rick Shortle, F.F 1600cc. Royale RP21.how exciting was that? My name, for the first time, in a race programme.

David and I repaired the car in time to have our final test session, which went ok, no damage so we only had to get it ready for the first race, in four days time.

We arrived at Brands on the Saturday morning, it was a two day meeting, day one would be qualifying, for grid positions for the race on Sunday, we didn't really have a clue what to do, we pulled our race car around the paddock looking for somewhere to park, and ended up next to a team that seemed very friendly and helpful, I explained to them it was my first race, would they mind guiding me in the right direction, on what to do, they were brilliant, and I must say it helped to take away all the anxiety, they even gave a hand to check my car over, before I took it to scrutineering, which is where it is looked over for legality and safety, we got through that, now waited to be called up over the tannoy system, to make our way to the collection area ready for our timed practice.

The Team next to us said don't worry we will tell you when it's time to go, so we just kicked our heels, and waited, deep down I was shitting myself, but excited at the same time, I heard us being called up for qualifying, I got into my car and followed our helpful neighbours up to the collection area, there must have been at least thirty cars all parked up, we seemed to sit there for an eternity, I could hear the cars out on the circuit qualifying for another race, the noise and tyre squealing was very loud, which made me feel even more nervous, we were beckoned through the tunnel to the pit lane, were we all parked up, one behind the other, in readiness to go out onto the circuit, as we sat there a marshal was making his way up the pit lane checking the cars, when he got to me, he asked me to pull my car out of the line, as he would like a word, I duly did this, he leaned over and asked where are the rest of my belts,? I explained that they were the only belts I had, and that I had bought it from someone that used to race it, so I couldn't understand why there is a problem, he explained, I do not have any crutch belts, they are the ones that go between your legs then clip into the central locking button along with the shoulder straps. He apologised. then said sorry no crutch belt no practice, I drove back to the paddock got out of the car, absolutely distort. Loaded the car up and went home, I phone the chap up that sold us the car, my intentions was to have a right go at him, when I explained, he said, look under the seat, the crutch straps were there, somehow we must have fed them back through the seat when we were cleaning it, dear oh dear what a couple of blithering idiots we are?

So hello good bye first race, at this rate we could turn out to be a bit of a laughing stock, our second race was only slightly more successful, we managed to qualify, twenty six out of twenty eight, not good but not last, got onto the starting grid, again the marshal was checking the cars, we were pulled off, only to be told we had a wheel nut missing, if it wasn't so funny I would have cried, but look on the bright side, things are getting better, rather than worse, David for whatever reason was quite philosophical about it, which was a bonus, as I really wasn't ready for any flack from him, I think he knew that anyway.

We decided to flog the RP21 and look for something else, there was a guy named Tim Lee Davey, he was in a TV show, call the Big Time, he went on to win the Dunlop Autosport Star of Tomorrow Championship, driving a car call a Tiga, we decided to look through the Autosport to see if one of those was up for sale, we found one, bought it and decided to take it to Tiga Racing to be checked over, they gave it the thumbs up, so we were quite upbeat.

I raced the Tiga at Brands a few times, and even though the plastering business was still going well, trying to race a car even on a small budget like us, costs a fortune, I told David that I couldn't afford it anymore, and have decided to put the car up for sale, we were both bitterly disappointed but what could I do, I put it up for sale in the Autosport in the hope I would sell it and salvage some money.

Chapter 14.
Enter Getem Racing

I remember vividly! sitting at the bottom of my stairs, when the phone rang, I answered it, a chap the other end said, it that Rick Shortle, I said yes, he said, are you the one that has a Tiga up for sale, yes I am, thinking, he was enquiring about it, he then went on to say, I do hope you're not thinking of packing up, I explained that I was, because it was getting far too expensive, and that David and myself just didn't have enough knowledge to carry on. He went onto say that his name was Martin Down of Getem Racing, he was the person that gave help and advise on our very first race day, his driver Andy Best had seen me race, and although I wasn't that quick, he felt given the right opportunity I could be quite good, he continued to say that his driver, was going to retire at the end of the season, and would I like to pop up and see him for a chat, I of course said yes, and went to see him that very day, I called David, telling him that I think I have been offered a drive in FF 1600. David being David said something like, you got no chance, which brought me down to earth a bit, but nothing ventured nothing gained, off I went to meet Martin Down.

Martin lived in New Ash Green, just a couple of miles away from Brands Hatch, it was early evening when I arrived, I knocked on the door to be met by his wife Judy, I explained who I was and she told me, he was in the garage at the bottom of the garden, I tapped on the side door, then pushed it open, to find Martin in his overalls working on his race car, he went on to explain his history, they had been building FF 1600 single seater race cars, for quite a number of years, and although they were a small team, building their own car, it was competitive, and sadly the first elusive win was still beckoning.

I was gobsmacked at the difference between David and myself, when preparing a race car, it had no comparison, Martin spent most of the evening just answering all my questions, it was mainly about the car, such as what is camber/caster/toe in/toe out/tyre pressures/ride heights. We seemed to hit it off immediately, and before he said anything, about what I was supposed to be there for, I knew that I would be racing his car.

Martin said, ok this is why I want to talk to you, how would you like to have a test in the Getem? Then afterwards we can discuss to see if you would like to take this any further, I jumped at the chance, I stayed with Martin in his garage until quite late, he shook my hand, and said he would call me, as soon as he can get booked in for a test session, at Brands. With that I left and drove home on cloud nine.

The next day I called David, he was very surprised at the outcome, but still the pessimistic sod he is, just said you better do the business then, although he was like that, through all the early days, his attitude helped to drive me on.

Martin rang a couple of days later, to give me the date for testing, I couldn't wait, and I think David deep down was chuffed at our luck too. It seemed strange going to Brands without the race car in tow, with the knowledge that there would already be a car waiting for me, we found Martin with his trusted helper Ken, who we soon nicknamed just a thought Ken, already working on the car, it was fantastic, something I couldn't have dreamt of in a million years, ok it's a very small team, that run a car they build themselves, but to us, an unbelievable stroke of luck, and as David quite rightly said, all I have to do now, is do the business.

Martin asked me to get in the car, so he could adjust the seat, pedals and gear change, which is situated on the right hand side in a single seater, once comfortable they did all sorts of things, such as put it on a flat area so the ride height can be checked, I was feeling important already.

Once they were happy with everything we made our way down to the pits, I was driving the Getem for the first time, but not as yet out on the circuit, once over, and parked up in the pit lane Martin asked me to get out, so we could have a chat, although we had already been through it, Martin suggested we go over it again, I listened intently, as I wanted to learn as much as I could.

Over the tannoy, they announced that practice had begun, Martin told me to take it steady for a few laps, at this stage I had nothing to prove, so I did exactly what he said, the car felt great, after about eight laps Ken gave me the in board, this was to ask how I felt, and do a systems check, I was fine, Martin showed me my lap times and without even trying I was as fast as I had ever been in the Tiga, naturally it made me feel great, David was at bottom bend with our stop watch, so we knew if there was any skull dugery with their times, but now that I know them, they would never tell you fibs to make you feel better, by doing something like that, by the end of testing I was within a second of the best time of the day, fantastic. We helped Martin and Ken load up, they suggested we went to the Kentagon for a drink and chat, I didn't know what to expect, and all I knew was that I wanted to drive for Getem Racing. We sat down and they got out the lap times, compared them with other drivers, and explained how I had done, what impressed them the most was, my peripheral vision, Martin has always said I had good peripheral vision, and my lap time were all within a couple of tenths of each other, and something I maintained to do throughout my racing career.

He asked me what I thought of the car, well what could I say, apart from how good it was, Martin said he would like me to drive for him next year, he understood I couldn't afford much, so he put an offer on the table, which was, if I would be prepared to put the money I get from the sale of the Tiga into Getem Racing, he will run me for a complete championship next year, but as it was a hands on team, he expected me to help as much as I could, well, I snatched his hand off, we shook on the deal, and that was it, I had just become a works driver for Getem Racing, it was only August, next year seemed so far away.

No way would I be able to keep away from Getem Racing, so I called Martin and asked if I could pop up now and again, to help him in the garage, he was more than delighted that I wanted to help, I needed to be involved with the building of next year's car, my car, which would be the GD113. I spent many hours at Martin's, and over the next two or three years, it must have mounted up to thousands, but it was something I wanted to do, to me the more time I spent with Martin the better I would get.

During the winter, it was all hands to the fore, it gave me a chance to get to know the team, which consisted of Martin Down, Team Principal, Ken just a thought Baker, Ken was Martins Brother-in-Law, and me, yes that was it, probably one of the smallest, if not the smallest works team in the country. Martin was the designer and builder, he had so many good ideas, obviously money was the issue, and although I was a works driver, we still had to keep within budget, they managed to do this by making everything they possibly could themselves, and even the bodywork was made from extremely thin plywood.

It was amazing to see the construction of my car coming together slowly but surely, Ken was on hand to help, although at times he was a pain in the arse, and he would agree with that, his input was very invaluable, sometimes he maybe just observing then all of a sudden he would say,

Martin, just a thought, don't you think it maybe better this way etc, that's where Ken just a thought Baker derives from, and I bet he is still the same to this day, I do hope so. Martin would sometimes send Ken off with the most impossible of tasks, he would always return with at least three options. Ken loved an argument, but he only argued for what he considered worth arguing about, and boy could he argue, bless him, during my time with Getem Racing, any problem, it was always Ken, go and sort it.

Martin is so passionate for the racing, I have known him to work through the night to repair the car, so it is ready to race the next day, his attention to detail is amazing, he would always go that extra mile to get it right, he is the loveliest most caring person you could ever wish to meet, before too long I was not just part of the team, but part of the family.

I would spend all my spare time helping, which meant plastering all day, then every evening drive from Ashford to New Ash Green, I would get there about 7pm and help Martin until at least 11pm, five nights a week, if we had a race it was load up on a Friday night, in readiness for the race, which was normally every other week. I continued to do this for the entire time I was with Getem Racing.

Chapter 15.
1982 racing begins.

It was January 1982, we made plans to have our car ready for pre season testing by mid February, we still had so much to do, I was impatient and Martin knew that, he took time to reassure me that the car should be ready, we discussed what was the best thing to do, should we enter a championship as mentioned by Martin on that first day, or should we race at as many circuits as possible, to get some valuable circuit knowledge, and then enter the Dunlop Autosport Star of Tomorrow Championship, the following year, I thought option two was a much better idea, the pressure would be off, not to compete in such a highly prestigious championship, and being my first year of proper racing, it would probably be too tough for me anyway.

Martin true to his word got the car ready in time for some testing, we of course went to Brands, as it was just down the road and the only circuit I had ever driven round, the first test day was all about shaking the car down, making sure everything worked and nothing fell off, the car felt great, and although I was keen to go fast, I respected the fact that Martin, Ken and myself had spent so many hours building it, we came away on the first test day, quite happy, everything worked as it should, just a few alterations with the pedals etc.

We were back at Brands the following week, and I was allowed to open it up, by the end of the session my times far exceeded anything I had managed before, Andy Best their previous driver came along to help, he jumped in the car, and to my amazement couldn't better my time, I was ecstatic, David was there as well, we were all chuffed with progress.

During my first year with Getem Racing, I suppose the best way to sum things up was, I gave them an awful lot of work to do, before the year ended my speed wasn't questioned, it was the fact I couldn't finish the race, and nine times out of ten, the poor Race Car made its way home, with at least one if not two wheels hanging off, but Martin never once got disillusioned, Ken was Ken, and David was David, I remember getting hold of Alain Prost's book, reading it I could see myself, it mentioned the fact that, if you didn't crash, you weren't trying, something Prost said, happened to him in his early days, so I took that on board, with the hope it would all change for the best, towards the end of the year I started to stay on and get some reasonable results, something we sorely needed, although the year hadn't quite gone according to plan, we were all confident that next year would be much better, we shall see.

During the winter it was decided to upgrade what we already had, the car was quick, I was comfortable in the car, so it was daft to change things too dramatically.

Being a plasterer, I put to Martin the idea of trying to change the bodywork, as I said earlier it was made out of Plywood, I suggested changing to fibre glass, I reckoned with a bit of advise it could be done, we needed the materials to carry it out, so off I went to Strand Glass Fibre in Ashford, fortunately I knew the Manager, I approached him with a proposal, this was to be my first attempt at getting sponsorship, he was aware I had just started racing, so it wasn't exactly a cold sell, I came away with a great deal, Strand would not only supply us with everything we needed, but also gave us team overalls, in exchange for their name on the car.

Martin was delighted, so after many attempts we ended up with bodywork made out of glass fibre, and even if I say so myself, the car looked so much better.

Having successfully secured sponsorship, I decided to try and get more, my second attempt was slightly unusual, I had a van with a roof rack, and came up with the idea of screwing advertising boards along the sides, back and front, of the roof rack. I split the boards on the sides, so two separate companies could have a panel each, it was painted in their colours, had their logo and phone number on, fortunately for me I was friendly with the local restaurant, the Newchurch House Restaurant near Hythe, they liked the thought of being associated with a local Race Driver, and hoped it would bring them some business, once I had one name up, I decided to clean the van so it looked smart, then drive around to local businesses, trying to sell them the idea, and do you know it worked, before long I had sold all six spaces, not for a lot of money, but every bit helps, from then on in, I never let an opportunity of getting sponsorship slip by.

Apart from trying to get better at racing I was becoming more and more aware of the fact, that it was so important to make sure the public knew about your dreams, ambitions, whatever you want to call it, I then decided to get an article in the local newspaper, this again was my first attempt at doing anything like this, I called the Sports Editor at the Ashford Advertiser, and gave him my story over the phone, he was very keen to promote local up and coming Race Drivers, an appointment was made to come and see me, asked if I could have the race car there too, I made sure he had everything he needed, including all the trophies I had won in Motor Racing Stables, he took a great picture of me posing next to the car with all my trophies, the write up was much better than I expected, well they know how to put these things together, the Sports Editor told me to send in regular reports when I start racing again next year, he would do his best to put them in the sports section.

Although our year had been disappointing, I felt I had taken a big leap forward in the Motor Racing world. I'm sure you know it's a Sport for young lads with rich parents, or people with bottomless pockets, both of which I didn't have, I just had the knack of being able to warm to people and convince them to be part of the Team by way of sponsorship.

The new season was approaching, we had our car almost ready, Martin up to now would rebuild his own engine, which I thought he did very well, however he was a little concerned, he said no matter what he did to his engine, it would never be quite the match for an engine supplied by the race tuners such as Auriga, Minister, Scholar or Nelson, in FF 1600 they were the business and all the top drivers would use them. Martin felt it was time to go and see one of them, our choice was Minister Engines, based near Chatham, we spoke to Graham Fuller, the front Man, he liked the idea of a small works team trying to compete against the big guns, such as Van Diemen, and Reynard, he theirfore was more than keen to help, it was going to cost of course, but he promised us an engine as good as any out there, although it was going to cost an arm and leg, we knew we had to do it, and once you have the engine, it doesn't stop there, it has to be re- built at least twice a year, which didn't come cheap, so we bit the bullet and ordered an engine.

We had to wait a month for our engine, so the car just sat there waiting for what was hopefully the final piece of the jigsaw, that's if my driving was going to be anything liked we all hoped it would be. The engine arrived, we installed it fired it up, I was expecting to hear something special, it sounded just like the old one, Martin did his usual pressure test, and found it to be much better than anything he had built himself, so our hopes were high, the only thing to do now was to take the car to a specialist exhaust maker in London, they made exhausts for most race cars, I took the car as Martin was working, but we arranged to meet in London as he was working there that day.

After the exhaust was completed, I parked the car and trailer with the race car on, and waited for Martin to appear, I spotted him walking towards me, he had the Auto sport in his hand, and was grinning like a Cheshire cat, I wondered why, I got out to greet him, he said have a read, the page was opened with the Heading Dunlop Auto sport Star of Tomorrow Championship. It was an article on potential candidates to win the series, just below the heading was a picture, of me driving the Getem, with the words underneath, Rick Shortle, could be a likely contender to win the championship, in Martin Downs unique works Getem, I was amazed, ok I proved I was quick, but hardly finished a race last year, obviously they knew something I didn't know, my goodness, this write up boosted me, and my confidence, I now began to belief in myself, I brought myself a copy and couldn't wait to show David, he was surprised as well, he said we know you are quick, all you have to do, is bloody well finish, and as usual he was right.

Two of the Getem cars I raced in the early days

Early days with the Getem Team. From left to right

Me-Anne-Judie Down-Dee Baker-Martin Down-Ken Baker- Brother David.

Chapter 16.
1983 Dunlop Autosport Star of Tomorrow Championship.

This year was a fantastic year, I hardly ever finished out of the top four, I won three races, and hardly ever crashed, I had gone through another big barrier, I think with any sport you go through barriers, you seem to struggle at the same pace, do all the same things wrong, then all of a sudden for whatever reason, you seem to go through that barrier, and just get better. I finished third in the championship, and felt as if I had joined that elusive club, I could win races, I was as much pleased for Martin, and Just a thought Ken, they had been waiting much longer than me for their first win, this was only my second proper year, and I was winning races.

Apart from the elation of winning, going to all the circuits, having so much fun was all part of making this year so special, as a small team, we didn't have the big expensive motor homes, we slept in a tent, which in its self was a great and very funny experience, Martins two boys, Nathan and Jason, and just a thought Ken's boy Simon, would come with us on most occasions, Ken would make his Son put his pajamers on before getting into bed, and you're not going to believe this, but Ken would sleep with his head outside the tent, because he liked the fresh air, he always wore his woolly hat. David and I would be in hysterics; secretly hoping a dog might come along in the middle of the night and cock his leg up.

I suppose it was always Ken making the entertainment, on more than one occasion as were driving to the circuit, he would get his road map out, and say, just a thought Martin, take the next left it's a short cut, and more times than not it was, but when it wasn't we would end up anywhere, Martin never got flustered, he took it all in his stride.

Martin's Boys, always sat in the back with me, they were very young then, but well behaved, I would say a little ditty which made them laugh, it went like this, Dib, Dib, Dib, Dib, Dob, Down with your Trousers and out with your Wallet, silly I know but they loved it.

I was still plastering, which became more and more difficult, trying to fit it in with going to Martins, and then going all over the country racing, it had to be done as this was my only form of income, during 1983, I did a plastering job for a chap named John Weir, he had an Accident repair business in Ashford, as usual if I get a sniff that someone is interested in my racing, I try to capitalize on it, he explained that he couldn't help much, but he would spray our chassis and bodywork, whenever we needed it done, this was great, another thing the team didn't have to worry about, John always showed an interest, and one day he called me, to mentioned a friend of his, by the name of Brian Varney, he gave me his number and told me to get in touch with him, as it could be very beneficial Brian invited me over to his offices in Wye, near Ashford in Kent, which is just down the road from me, we had a meeting, and unbeknown to me, he had been following my progress in the Autosport all year, I recon John had mentioned it to him quite a while ago, and Brian being Brian had quietly followed my progress throughout the year, before making a decision to talk, Brian knew exactly how I did, we had a long talk, he seemed very pleasant, this meeting for potential sponsorship, wasn't like any other, to be honest I didn't know what to expect, he handed me a cheque for some tyres and said he would keep an eye on my progress.

Toward the end of 1983 Brian called me and suggested we meet up and have a meal, I recommended the Newchurch House Restaurant, well! They were an existing sponsor of mine. He told me to bring Anne along, as he was bringing his wife Judy, we had a lovely meal, not much was said, I was hoping he might be giving us further sponsorship, which I discovered a few days later he was, Brian went on to be a major sponsor of mine for several years, and I suppose it's true to say, without Brian, I certainly wouldn't have had the success that I achieved over the next few years, Brian was first and foremost a business Man, he became my Manager, and friend, he would organise, the press releases, talk to potential sponsors, pay the team, organise hospitality, in fact everything really, and to think about it, only three years ago I had put my Race Car up for sale because I had run out of money.

What a start for 1984, we not only have a good car with a good engine, and hopefully a good driver, but we also have the finances, roll on 198

Chapter 17.
1984 John Player Special Champion of Brands.

Expectation were sky high, pre season testing went without a hitch, both car and engine performed well, in testing I was quickest most of the time, so the word around the paddock was all about Rick Shortle and the Getem Down. GD114. My new major sponsor made time to come along to most test days, Brian had never done this sort of thing before, he's the type of chap that loves to be involved, I think it's very important to welcome sponsors along, so they get an idea of what happens behind the scenes, prior to the race, over the next few years, everybody got to know Brian, that's for sure.

On paper, 1984 looked as if it was going to be the best season so far, but although I was one of the quickest in the first few races I was unable to turn my speed into victory, however from race four something clicked, I seemed to go through another barrier, and from April through to September I was putting my car on pole most of the time, and winning most of the races, I was leading the Championship by quite a margin, I was quietly confident that this could be the year I would win my first Championship.

But unfortunately, fate has a habit, of turning everything upside down, it was about to do just that. I was still managing to be a plasterer, I had to really, as this was my only form of income. Still living in Sellindge. Which, is near Ashford, in Kent? One morning we were on our way to a plastering job in Folkestone, when I say we, I mean myself and plasterers mate Rob Wills, had only travelled about 4 miles, then as we were approaching a very sharp right hand bend a Land Rover came towards us on our side of the road, the last thing I remember is hearing this horrible metal to metal noise as he hit our car, head on, luckily for Rob it struck the front drivers side, which thankfully prevented Rob from getting injured. The moment he hit our car I went unconscious.

When I came round I was being tended to by the Flying Doctor, the Fire Service were present, I remember vividly calling my mate Rob over, saying Rob, I've been drinking, he said don't be daft, it's the gas and air they are giving you.

The Escort estate was in such a mess, they had to cut the back of the seat off, and remove the roof to get me out, it took an hour and a half to extrude me from the car, in the meantime the Police had informed my wife Anne, I remember being taken to Ashford Hospital in excruciating pain, to cut a long story short, I had a smashed pelvis, and a broken femur, at the point where it joins the ball, that sits in the pelvis, this had to be screwed back together with a compression pin and plate, the plate was about 8 inches long, that had to be left in my leg to hold the two pieces of bone together for a year, then hopefully back for a minor operation to remove them. I spent about a month in hospital, and apart from concern over a very large swollen stomach, which was initially thought to have been something wrong with my spleen, and I understand can be quite dangerous, but thankfully discovered within a few days, it was due to the fact that I had cut my face quite badly, and swallowed a lot of blood, this stayed in my stomach until I was sick, the blood just flew out, it seemed like bucket loads, what a relief, worry gone, belly flat, it was quite funny, prior to that, the Nurses would measure my stomach three times a day, and instead of letting me lay on the tape measure, which would prevent me from getting pain from them Having to slide the tape under my, bearing in mind my pelvis was shot to pieces, it was something I dreaded. Apart from that it was quite a laugh, I was amazed at the number of drivers and spectators that came along to visit me, in those days, you were allowed as many visitors as you wanted, I think the most I had at any one time was 15. I hate to say this but its true, visitors can be a complete pain in the arse, all the patient wants to do is just lay there and get better.

Unfortunately my attempt to win the Championship ended there and then, I was unable to take any further part, which was a shame, as I was leading the championship by quite a margin. It would have been fantastic to have given Martin Down and Ken just a thought Baker a Championship in their car. Racing was now well and truly in my blood, I couldn't wait to at least go to Brands and show my face, after all, the drivers and fans had been great, this really did give me a boost, I was already getting impatient, all I wanted was to get back in a race car.

So 1984 didn't quite go to plan, but as I rested at home in bed, my Manager Brian Varney was beavering away trying to sort things out for 1985. In the meantime, I received a letter from John Webb, the owner of Brands Hatch Circuits, saying he would like to discuss the possibility of me becoming a race instructor, to think I was a pupil at the very same a mere four years ago.

In those days you had to be invited as well as have a good racing pedigree, I was beside myself, this was a fantastic opportunity, not only to race cars but also to be able to make a living out of instructing, Mr Webb was very approachable, and to be fair it wasn't an interview, just a chat, I think he wanted to know if I was the right sort of person for the job.

I got an immediate start, Tony Lanfranci was still in charge, my job for the first three days was making tea for everybody, and I wasn't too proud, because I was keen as mustard to learn. In those days it was fantastic fun, but at the same time, we made sure that everyone was given the best tuition possible, as I said earlier, back then, it was a real racing school, teaching those with any potential, to become race drivers, mind you, very few actually made it, I know myself how difficult it was going to be, many over the years ask me what it takes to become a race driver, I just said, you have to be single minded, focused, believe in yourself , and prepared to sacrifice everything, then don't bother, unless you are rich or your family have money to burn, I also told them something that I believe, and that is if you want something bad enough, it will happen, a philosophy I still believe in to this day.

Allthough a great year things didn't always go to plan.

Chapter 18.
1985 FF 1600 RAC Championship.

I was aware that Brian had been having talks with leading FF1600 manufactures Van Diemen, Reynard, and others, regarding a works drive, these people were the big boys, and up to now I had been beating them in a one off car, this gave me so much creditability, nobody expected me to be as competitive, yet alone, win against them. In the end we chose to become an assisted works driver for Reynard, run by Mike Parks, alongside Tim Jones, the Son of Legendary Brands Hatch Commentator, Brian Jones.

With success, become decisions, some of which are not that pleasant, I now had to carry out one of the most unpleasant things, I had ever had to do, and this was to tell Martin Down that I no longer wish to drive his beloved Getem GD FF1600. This was heart wrenching, at the time I broke the news to him, I was unable to drive, as I was still getting over the road accident, so he came to see me at Sellindge, I remember him arriving, I could tell he was excited about 1985, I knew it was important to tell him before he got too involved with his plans, I just blurted it out, Martin was so upset, he tried to get me to change my mind, I now couldn't make a decision like that, I had a major sponsor/manager, plus I had to move forward, Martin left totally deflated, I felt the same.

At least I knew that Martin was not the kind of person to hold a grudge, in fact I think he was chuffed to bits, that he had produced a car and driver, to get so much attention, I will always be eternally grateful to Martin and Ken, for giving me the chance to drive their car, without them I would not have been racing, so thanks Martin and just a thought Ken, with that in mind, and a couple of months before the 1985 testing begins, I was quite confident, that that it would all blow over well before then.

To me this was the biggest challenge of my short motor racing career; I was now a works assisted driver for one of the best manufactures in FF1600. I was racing in the most prestigious FF1600 Championship in the world, against the best drivers in the world, and theirfore the potential of becoming a Formula One Driver, this year's Championship had the likes of Damon Hill, Eddie Irvine, the late, Roland Ratzenberger, to name just a few. Need I say any more?

Unfortunately, the all new Reynard never showed the promise, the manufactures said it would, Tim and I struggled to be competitive, as did all the other Reynard drivers, Brian was getting impatient and expected more, and by March we withdrew from the Championship and left Mike Parks Racing.

The uncompetitive Reynard 85.

Within no time at all, Brian had sealed a deal to move up a formula, to FF2000 with Rob Cresswell Racing. driving a 1984 Reynard, Rob had already produced several Champions he was always someone I had respected as a racing engineer.

The Reynard FF 2000

*My Manager-Sponsor, Brian Varney, and Anne proudly
pose for a photo, with myself in the car.*

It was decided that we entered a few races here and there,
Silverstone, Oulton Park, Donnington, just to get used to
driving a racing car that had wings, and wide slick tyres
just like a F1 car

I seemed to be competitive straight away; Rob felt it suited
my smooth driving style.

At the end of the year, we entered the BBC Winter Grandstand series, at Brands Hatch, I finished third overall.

In between these races, I entered the Formula Ford Festival at Brands Hatch, with Rob Cresswell, in a 1984 Reynard, and not the ill fated 1985 model, this is the big one, the show case for F.Fords, Drivers come from all over the world, there are up to 280 drivers all trying to win the final, it is run over three days, and is without doubt, the most competitive and thrilling race meeting to watch.

My 1984 Reynard, number 1 another win

Leading Damon Hill in the 1985 Formula Ford Festival.

Although I didn't win the Festival or even make the final, it was without doubt as far as I'm concerned, the best I have ever driven, I was on fire.

The family were there Anne, daughters Tina and Julia, my biggest critic, Brother David, and of course, Manager Brian Varney. All standing on a porta cabin roof, shoulder to shoulder with Damon Hill's crew, at the back of the garages in the centre, they had a prime spot, to watch the racing. I can remember seeing them waving furiously as I passed by after each race had ended, even David was over the moon with my performances, something I'm sure you have realised by now is an unusual occurrence

Getting back to Rob, I had so much faith in him, if he had said, drive through that brick wall, I would have done, when testing with Rob he was infuriating, any adjustment he did on the car, he would check double check then check again, we could be sitting in the pit lane for what seemed like hours, and perhaps we would only do a few laps at the time, but boy oh boy, those few laps were always fast, so in the end I got to understand him, and became more tolerant. Knowing that the car he gave me to drive, would be as good as any car out there.

I went out in the semi finals, John Booth, now the Team principal of the Virgin Formula One Team, in his time a good peddler, he out braked himself, hitting me up the back, and punted me off on the entry to Druids Hairpin, I was just a passenger in my car, I think I took at least half a dozen drivers out with me, I managed to limp back to the pits, oh well that's motor racing as they say, but I often think how I may have got on, if I wasn't so unceremoniously knocked off by John.

With any race season, it's not what you do throughout the year but it's what you do at the end that counts, and although I never made the final, I certainly left my mark at the 1985 Formula Ford 1600 Festival. I got good press and exposure, my confidence was through the roof, and I knew that 1986 was going to be a very good year, whatever we do.

There is nothing better than winning

Soon to become my best buddie Chris Hall on the right.

Chapter 19
1986 FF 1600 Champion of Brands.

This was destined to be the most successful year to date; I was staying with Rob Cresswell Racing, and driving the fantastic 1984 Reynard, that gave me so much success in the Festival. I was in another gear, and was brimming in confidence, just had this inner self belief, I had never felt this way before, I can remember waking up on race day, looking at the list of drivers, and not worrying about my opposition, just thinking how much I would out qualify them by, I often wonder if that was arrogance, or just confidence, whatever it was, it worked for me.

I loved that car

Let the Championship begin, after finishing second to my main rival Chris Hall, in the first race, I went on to win nearly every race, until I had a bad accident two thirds of the way through the season, it was on the Grand Prix Circuit at Brands, going through Dingle Dell, which completely wrecked the car.

Brian was on the phone talking to the manufactures, trying to get a free car, we were in a strong position to get one, as I was firm favourite, to take the title, so whatever make I was driving at the end of the year, that

Manufacturer could claim, the Championship was achieved in their car, we ended up with a Van Diemen, which was used only once in the Race of Champions at the 1985 British Grand Prix Silverstone.

We swapped to the Van Dieman 85, front row of the grid number 130

Rob being Rob wasn't happy with the preparation, he spent hours upon hours making sure it was as good as it could be, we took it to a Brands test session, and it wasn't long before I was on the pace, but something wasn't quite right, none of us knew what it might be, I do know Rob wasn't happy, he hated things not being correct, our times got better and better, I was feeling more confident but not 100% happy, I just felt because it was a different make of car I needed time to get used to it, last outing of the day, as I was turned into Paddock Hill Bend, it all of a sudden swapped ends, I ended up going into a tyre wall backwards, at the bottom of the Hill, doing about 90mph, I knew it was going to hurt so I braced myself, sure enough it did hurt, I ended up with three cracked ribs and whiplash, which is painful, they put me in a neck brace then took me to St Mary's Hospital in Swanley. The whiplash was so painful, even when I blinked my eyes it seemed to hurt, there I was another accident, and again sidelined for a couple of races, Rob found out that the chassis was cracked right under the driver's seat, and it wasn't until he had stripped the car completely down, did they discover the cracked chassis, Brian managed to get a new chassis, free of charge from Van Diemen, Rob and Dave spent a couple of days at the Van Diemen's Factory, rebuilding the car, I was out of action for three weeks which meant I had to miss a couple of races, unfortunately with the points system, I dropped from the top of the points table, instead of leading the Championship I went down to fourth, and although I won first time out against my main rival, I somehow never felt the same again, in fact I found it an uphill struggle to stay competitive, it just seemed the harder I drove the slower I got, it wasn't until the Championship was finished that we discovered the differential, had a different ratio to the one used in Formula Ford, that immediately answered our questions why we had no straight line speed, I still don't know to this day why we ended up with a diff with the wrong ratio. Something, fishy there.

Anyway I didn't win the Championship, I lost it by one measly point, but it was a fantastic year, I was awarded the BRSCC, Post Two Marshalls Trophy, for not only being a good driver but for also giving value for money throughout the season, I was honoured to accept the Trophy, my name is on that Trophy for ever, along with some great drivers, including a couple of Formula One Drivers.

Posing with the Post Two Marshalls Trophy (pi__c__

I felt my time racing Formula Ford was over, and I should pursue another formula.

Chapter 20.
My remaining years as a race driver

Now you have an idea of my racing, I have decided not to continue with a year by year account, but to condense the final years to a single chapter, as I realise not everyone enjoys motor racing, and the last thing I want to do is bore some of you senseless. In 1987 I contested the Sports 2000 Championship with the Royal Works Team, I finished third overall, and thoroughly enjoyed the racing, it was far more sedate than Formula Ford, and to be fair, one season was quite sufficient. I still couldn't resist having the odd outing in a Formula Ford, just for fun, I entered a few celebrity races, and in a pro celebrity race I broke the lap record in a Ford Escort by half a second, previously held by none other than ex Formula One Driver John Watson.

Unfortunately my Manager Brian Varney decided that he no longer wished to continue as a Manager and sponsor, I was obviously devastated, as up to now I didn't have any concerns about finding the money, now I was back on my own. I had nothing but gratitude for Brian, without him I would never have had so much success, although I was without finance I still felt I could continue, for the next couple of years I did the odd race here and there, including the Willhire 24hr Race in a Cosworth Sierra, at Snetterton, my Co Driver was none other than Tony Lanfranci, yes the very same, the man I had to report to, when I climbed up those stairs, for the first time at the Brands Hatch Motor Racing Stables, how fantastic was that?

The Cosworth Sierra I raced, along with Tony Lanfranci at the Willhire 24hrs. Snetterton

I kept plugging away trying to secure sponsorship, and like I said earlier, If you want something bad enough you will get it. As with most things, there is always an element of luck, but you must capitalize on it, I was instructing at Brands one day, on a Corporate event, now these were always a good hunting ground for sponsorship, although we were all told that it is a no go area, on no account, must we prostitute ourselves for money, to go motor racing, but there is always a way round this, if the guest gets talking, and starts to ask questions about your racing career, you have to tell them, and if they ask about cost etc it would be rude not to answer, and sometimes they may even ask if you are looking for sponsorship, this very rare, and most of the time, it never comes to fruition, but it must be pursued.

On this particular day I met a chap call Jeremy Axworthy, he couldn't stop talking, and couldn't stop telling me what he has done and what he intends to do etc. But thats fine you soon learn never to disagree with a potential sponsor, Jeremy put his money where his mouth was, and immediately sponsored me with a road car, in fact he went on to supply me with a car for the next three years, so it was worth having to put up with his nonstop banter, on the odd occasion. But most importantly he went on to introduce me to a potential sponsor, they were a couple of high flyers, just opening a mortgage broker business, and looking for exposure.

I arranged a meeting, it went well. but before they committed themselves, they would like a taster, so I suggested they came along to Brands, I would put their logo on the race car free of charge; they could bring a few guests along, and hopefully get the bug. Although it didn't happen overnight, a sponsorship deal was struck; their company sponsored me for the next three years in the Honda CRX Challenge. Which is a one make saloon car series, featuring the latest Honda CRX Hatch Backs, the racing was fast and furious, the first few races was a big eye opener, having been used to open seater race cars, I was still programmed as a Formula Ford driver, this was obviously wrong, it's all about panel bashing and god knows what else, once I realised that's the way to go I was fine, these one make saloon drivers, are a specialist lot, it was hard at first to understand how to drive these little front wheel drive cars, being a FF 1600 you have to get into the corner as quick as possible, front wheel drive saloon cars are different, but slowly, and slower than I had expected, I began to get on the pace, my first season was a learning year, I finished 10th overall, my second year was much better, no wins but a few podiums and a 6th place overall, my third and final year was fantastic, three wins help me net 3rd place, in the Championship. Without doubt once you get the hang of driving a front wheel drive car on the limit, it is almost, yes almost as enjoyable as racing a FF1600. It was now 1994, I had been racing for over 12 years, and in that time I have met so many fantastic people, I have made so many friends, drivers, spectators, people in the Media, and of course the Marshalls, who do a fantastic job, they truly are the unsung heroes.

The Honda CRX Team. My car is far right.

Mainly I suppose due to lack of sponsorship, I decided to call it a day, and hang my helmet up, I have to admit that it was extremely hard not to try and raise sponsorship, and get back in a car, and on the odd occasion I have weakened, hired a race car and gone testing, just to see if I was still on or near the pace, the last time I sat in a race car, was at Oulton Park, in the year 2000, it was on a test day, I was driving a Renault Clio, and by the afternoon I was quick enough to have qualified on the 2nd second row. At the time it gave me such a buzz, I felt the yearning to want to race, but once I was away from the track and on my way home, the buzz went, so I knew, in the future, if I decide to have another go, I must treat it as just a bit of fun, and I also knew deep down, I could never be as competitive as I was before, and I'm not the sort of person to run around the back just for fun, so hopefully that is the end of what I would describe as a chequered career.

Chapter 21.
New horizons

Going back a bit, it was 1984 when I had decided to pack up plastering, and concentrate on being a racing instructor, I was getting so much work, not only as an Instructor at Brands, but travelling all over the country, and sometimes to France, Italy, Spain and Germany, to the race tracks, for major car manufactures such as Audi-BMW-Ford-Nissan-Toyota and Alfa Romeo. Our job was to drive the guests, mainly sales staff, around the circuits at speed, just to give them and idea of what it is like, also to show the car off, and then hopefully they would be more upbeat about their product, and be able to sell with far more enthusiasm. They were great years I made so many friends, one in particular, I haven't mentioned him much, his name is Chris Hall, Chris was a fantastic Formula Ford driver, he drove for Jamun Racing, he was my biggest rival during my FF 1600 days at Brands, most of the time it was either Chris winning, or me winning, for whatever reason, we hated each other, he would spread rumours that my car was illegal, I would do the same about him. But once we stopped racing against each other, we became the best of friends. Chris now lives in Florida, he must have been over there for at least 15 years, he's married, with two children, a girl and boy, he's living the dream, as they say, he is still racing and doing good, we have been to see him a few times, before he left England we would travel the country together, on the Manufactory days, we had so many good times, funny, after we stopped racing against each other, we became the best of buddies, and we always will be.

Another chap that has helped me over the years, was Ken Hall, Ken is the type of fella, no matter what troubles he may have, he always had time to help and advise me, thanks Ken. I made many friends in this industry, sadly far too many to mention.

In 1986 I became a Chief instructor, which meant not only a pay rise, but also could pick and choose what we did, part of this position included, teaching new instructors how to do the job properly, at the time it was just myself and now, best buddie, Chris Hall, that were Chief Instructors. We also got chosen to instruct top Celebrities, MP's, etc, and over the years, I had the privilege to meet and instructed so many famous people, such as, Frankie goes to Hollywood - Mark Thatcher - Sylvia Simms -Bobby Moore (a fantastic bloke) - Eddie Kid Stirling Moss - Jackie Stewart - half the 1990 England Football Team - Chief Minister of the Isle of Man – Derek Daley – to name but a few.

In June 1989 Chris and I spent the day with actors Stuart Wolfenden and Michael Le Vell, both better known for their parts in Coronation Street, Stuart is no longer in the

Street, but Michael, better known as Kevin Webster is still going strong with his garage, part of the story line in 1989 was about Kevin and Stuart going Banger Racing, ITV strongly advised that they visit the Race School at Brands, to help them understand a bit more about racing.

Stuart and Michael Actors from Coronation Street, getting words of advise, from Chris Hall and myself at Brands Hatch.

Chris and I spent the whole day looking after them, we had such a laugh, they were real down to earth people, and once the instruction was over, we spent a couple of hours in the Thistle Hotel downing a few drinks and talking about the day, both of them were buzzing, great fun, great memories. We ended up getting great coverage in the TV Times, with pictures of Chris and myself giving them instruction, my Mum was so proud, she put a copy of the TV Times in the back window of her car and even opened it, at the relevant page, bless her.

I also had the privilege to be asked if I would instruct a chap by the name of Bob Mathews, apparently he was an Olympic medallist for running, I thought no problem there, should be a breeze, however Bob was just a bit different, he was Blind.

Blind Athelete, Bob Mathews, being helped into the Racing Honda CRX, by my sponsor.

I had a chat with Bob as he sat all belted up in my Racing Honda CRX. The chat was just as much for me, as it was for him, I needed to know what type of instruction would be more beneficial, he felt the best way would be, to drive him round slowly for a few laps, and to explain how the track looked, what the bends were like, any trees, bridges, fences or buildings etc, as apparently, a blind persons hearing is far better than a normally sighted person, they can tell if they are near trees, bridges, buildings etc.

So I did just that, then after a few laps, Bob felt confident enough to drive me. We pitted and swapped places, it's quite strange, but I wasn't the least bit concerned, I just made sure I gave good slow instructions, basically the same as when I was driving, but this time it was Bob at the wheel, we did three full laps of Brands, Bob reached a speed of 45mph down the main straight, he even managed to leave the circuit and drive back into the pit lane, Bob was amazing, we then swapped over, so I could drive him for a couple of fast laps which he loved.

It was now 1990. I had been an instructor at Brands for 7 years, the whole concept had changed, and although it was still great fun for those that attended, it was no longer a stepping stone for any aspiring race drivers, I enjoyed it more, when it was for the budding racer, basically I was getting a bit tired of the job, and to think back when I started, to me it was the best job in the world, my how things change, I didn't have a clue what to do, other than less instructing and more dealership days, all over the Country, and sometimes abroad, I wasn't unhappy just looking for a change, then hey presto, I happened to buy the Autosport, and as I was flicking through it, I noticed in the Classified Adds section under job vacancies, a position for a Circuit Manager, at Snetterton has become available, which is part of Brands Hatch Circuit Ltd. As is Oulton Park and Cadwell Park.

I chewed this over and decided I would have a word with a chap by the name of Richard Green, he was the Business Development Manager for Brands Hatch Circuits Ltd, I knew him well, and fortunately he was based at Brands.

I popped in to see him on my dinner break, explaining I had seen the Snetterton Circuit Managers position advertised, and I was interested, but would like his honest opinion, if he felt I would be suitable for the job, he had no qualms, in being pleased that I was interested, and advised me to apply for the job.

I decided to apply, I had nothing to lose, within a few days I had a telephone call from Nicola Foulston, the new Circuit owner, she would like to see me regarding my application for the Managers job. I went along and put my case forward, why I would make a good Manager, and also stressed, that I still wished to continue racing She asked several questions, then advised me I would hear in a week or so, to be honest I never expected to get the job, and in a way it made me relaxed during the interview, I knew I came across quite well. So all I had to do was wait to hear.

To be honest I never gave it much thought, until a week or so later when the letter arrived, it was a posh white envelope with the words embossed on the front, The Office of the Chief Executive. I knew this was either going to be yes or know, and although I felt I knew the answer, I still didn't want to open the envelope, it was a bit like opening a bank statement, knowing that you were overdrawn and didn't want to know, I

gently opened the envelope then even more slowly pulled the letter out, it took forever to pluck up the courage to unfold the letter, I began to read the letter, not taking my eyes off the line I was reading, as I didn't want to read the next line, it didn't take long to realise which way this was going, it just said, dear Rick, we are delighted, with that I knew I had the job, and just as importantly, there wouldn't be a problem for me to continue racing, I couldn't believe it, I must have read the letter twenty times, and wondering why the hell did I get the job, for a couple of days I was in a bit of a daze, I sent off my acceptance for the position and waited to hear what the next step would be.

Everything seemed to be moving at 100 miles an hour, Nicola wanted me to take over at Snetterton as soon as possible, the existing Manager was going to run Oulton Park, and they didn't want to leave a Circuit without a Manager, I'm not sure how soon it actually was, but believe me it wasn't long at all, we had our own bungalow at Sellindge, this had to go on the market, I couldn't commute, as Snetterton was over 120 miles away, fortunately the job came with accommodation, which was a spacious bungalow at the entrance to the circuit, lucky for us, both Tina and Julia had flown the nest, so we only had ourselves to sort out.

Up to now I had not received any induction, or training whatsoever, and believe it or not, apart from one afternoon meeting the staff, and telling them what I would expect from them, followed by the Saturday before we moved up, meeting the existing Manager David Ross, whilst a race meeting was going ahead, David went through a few things, I was totally confused, didn't have a clue what to do, he buggered off and left me to it,

the minute he left, I had a message over the radio that the toilets were blocked, and could I get someone to sort them, I had no idea what to do, but somehow I got it fixed, and I tell you I was bloody relieved when the meeting had finished. Later that evening, I remember standing in the middle of the Circuit thinking this is all mine, what the hell have I done?

Come Monday morning, I have to look as if I know what I am doing, I decided the best way forward, was to go around the circuit, chat with all the staff individually, find out their job description, ask a few questions, basically try to get an understanding on what they did, because I had not got a clue who did what, there are around 20 full time workers. The Circuit boasts a Licensed Pub, First Aid Centre, Restaurant, Racing School, and 4 Industrial Units leased by Racing Teams. So roll on Monday morning.

Chapter 22.
Snetterton Motor Racing Circuit.

Between the baptism of fire on the Saturday and Monday morning, we managed somehow to get moved in and sorted on the Sunday, we had put most of our own furniture in storage, as the bungalow was furnished, being busy on the Sunday was ideal, at least it took our minds off my first day in charge. We slept well Sunday night.

Monday morning, my first port of call was the office, which is situated less than thirty feet from our bungalow, I must admit to being extremely nervous, the office is the heart of the circuit, the staff are paramount to the success of the circuit, we had three fulltime office staff plus myself. On reception was Maria and Pauline, in the back was Georgina our fulltime bookkeeper, and myself, I was worrying unduly, the office girls were brilliant, and I have to say it wasn't just the first day, they were brilliant all the time, in particular Maria, she could have run that circuit herself, and I have no doubt that she was instrumental in getting me up to speed in such a quick time.

I did exactly what I had decided to do, go and speak to the staff individually, and it worked out much better than I expected, by the end of the day, I not only,, had a much better idea of the workings of the circuit, but also more importantly, got to know the staff, and each and every one of them was a character, with Norfolk people until they get your trust, you are an interloper, and when I first arrived, the rumour going around the circuit, was that I was here to close it down, as it was earmarked for a major housing development.

Although that was complete and utter rubbish, I had to work hard to convince them otherwise. My first port of call was to visit Betty her main assistant Hazel and crew, in the circuit restaurant named Tyrell's, after the Tyrell Formula One Team, the restaurant was a fairly new addition, it was only a couple of years old, and in comparison with most other circuits it was as good, if not better than most, Betty was a lovely Lady, and I think it was fair to say she was of generous proportions, they cooked fantastic breakfasts and dinners, Tyrell's was always spotless, and run extremely well, it was very important to spend time with her, listening to her problems and sometimes gripes about other staff, after a while I understood her and had my own way of keeping her sweet. That first morning I discovered that there was a rift between the Office and Tyrell's, which I discussed later with the office, to me, it seemed six of one and half a dozen of the other, I felt the way forward was to get them all together and thrash it out, we did just that, and although it didn't totally resolve the problems, it went a long way towards helping, at least both sides could see, they now had a Manager that at cares, and tries to do something about it.

I then went and had a chat with the maintenance staff run by Chris, his team included Mike and Bernie, no not (Winters) although at times they were hilarious, this colourful band of Men, were responsible for anything and everything, that was required to keep the circuit looking neat and tidy, Chris would pop to the office for instructions every morning at 9am, this was something I found relatively easy from day one, I would make a point of checking the circuit out at least once a day, and make notes of anything that required attention, I remember the first problem they had, it was to form new kerbing to the chicane, I found out that this should have been carried out weeks ago, but nobody had any idea how to do it, with my building experience it was something I understood how to do, so I decided to get myself into overalls and get it done, Chris and his crew were amazed, I think they expected me to be a bit different from that, we completed the kerbs in a couple of days, and from that day on, they knew I was able to understand what they did, and more importantly, probably knew more than they did about quite a few things, I met Margret the Manager of the circuit pub, she was a bit of a loner, and wasn't too much trouble, I always made sure I popped in on race days for a swift half, and a chat with her and the drivers.

Then there was Bob the fireman and Terry the resident Doctor, Bob and Terry were thick as thieves, Terry was very outspoken, but bloody good at his job, he also ran the control tower on general practice, which was five days a week, in an emergency you couldn't wish for two better blokes.

Snetterton was the busiest Racing Circuit in the Country, boasting each year, 180 test days, on the odd occasion, Formula One Team Lotus. Based at Hethel just up the road, would exclusively hire the track for a week at the time, their diver was Johnny Herbet, who I knew quite well, having raced against him in Formula Ford 1600. It also ran, about 40 Car meetings which included British Touring Cars, Formula 3000, and Formula Three Championships, as well as 35 Bike meetings a year, not forgetting about 20 Racing School days, so I had quite a lot on my plate.

Yes it was a massive task, but for whatever reason I took to it like a Duck to water, even Nicola Foulston was delighted with my progress, I think it was made easier by the fact that I knew most of the Teams and Drivers. I understood from a drivers perspective what was required.

Maintenance was easy, when we were busy preparing for a big meeting, to help out, I used to jump on the tractor during the evening, to mow acres of grass, something I loved doing, Anne would sit in the Grandstand at the Bomb hole, reading a book, the Bomb Hole is a corner named after a bomb that ended up there during the 2nd World War, we were so happy and contented, I was able to make improvements as long as they were not major, and in no time at all the circuit looked more colourful, tidier and all in all a better place to visit.

This all rubbed off on the Staff, they all seemed to have more of a spring in their steps, and after about six months, I knew the Staff were very happy with me as their Manager, the thing with Norfolk people, once you get to that stage they are your friends for life? It's a great feeling.

Being the Manager of a race circuit has its perks, we were always being invited to functions, Anne ended up with a wardrobe full of posh frocks for the occasions, going out never cost us a penny, on circuit there was a gang of Marshalls, that would go rabbit shooting some evenings, and when they were finished they would always drop us off a pair for our dinner, I was still racing in the Honda CRX Challenge, when the drivers from the Championship would test or race there, we would put a couple up overnight, it was great we were never short of friends, although to many, it may have looked like a lonely desolate place, especially when nothing was going on, and in the dead of night it was very eerie, but to us it was our home and an exciting place to live.

Every Sunday was a massive Market, just opposite our bungalow, as Manager it was under my umbrella, although I really didn't have much to do, it ran itself, we just took the rent, I would still walk round and have a chat with the stall holders, if I had to say what was the worst thing about living there, without doubt it was the whiff of burgers being cooked in what must have been oil that had long past its sell by date, it was awful.

We had settled in extremely well, I made my usual monthly trip to Brands, to attend the Managers Meeting,

I realise it was important to keep up with any changes, but to be honest, as with all these sort of meetings, they were bloody boring, I considered the topics of discussion were not worth talking about, but it had to be done, to be fair it was good when they went through things such as circuit budgets, and turnovers, I was always under budget, and above turnover, I got praised for that, but I was still glad when the meeting ended, the best thing about going to Brands, was nipping down to the circuit, to say hello to all the instructors, it was a change to get back to reality, and a nice way to end the day, even though I was a Manager. I still felt like an instructor, I enjoyed seeing the instructors and having a laugh, before making my journey back home to Snetterton.

My racing continued and was going very well, I think it was partly to do with the fact, that I was settled and relaxed, on the weekends I was racing, they sent a relief manager to be on hand, as most weekends there was a race meeting of some description or another, but to be fair, the meetings are run by the organising club such as the BRSCC or BARC, all we had to do was to make sure the circuit was ready, and things like radios etc were available, the restaurant, pub, and medical centre ran as per normal, by our able staff, Chris, Mick, and Bernie worked every weekend to look after things trackside, such as re building tyre walls and picking up vehicles that had crashed on the track, the staff had been doing this for years, so there was nothing to worry about.

Apart from all the normal issuesy you would expect with running something like this, everything went swimmingly,

My Mum and her Husband Reg, would visit quite a lot, they loved to wander round the market, and try to get a bargain or two, Mum always made sure to pop down to Tyrell's, for a breakfast, Betty always made a fuss of them.

I had been the Manager for a little over 18months, the circuit looked better than it had ever done before, I was loving my job, it wasn't unusual to work a 14 hour day, to me it wasn't work it was more like a hobby, so I was shocked when I was winding down in the office one evening, the fax machine began to receive a document, to my horror it was to inform me that the Chief Executive of Brands Hatch Circuit Ltd. had decided that I shall cease racing forthwith, they felt it was regarded as being too risky, for top Management to participate in dangerous sports, such as Motor Racing, I was extremely upset and in a dilemma, for a start I couldn't pack up racing, even if I wanted to, I had sponsors that were signed up for the year, and quite frankly I wasn't ready to stop racing anyway, I gave it plenty of thought, and decided to write and put my case forward, explaining the reasons why being a race driver, is good for the circuit, I had already proved that, to me it was perfect, a racing driver running a race circuit, I knew firsthand what the drivers wanted, I was on talking terms with them all, and with my construction experience as well, I reckoned it was a perfect mix.

I soon got a reply, stating that was the decision, and I would not be an exception to the rule. Although I truly didn't want to leave, my draw to racing was still too strong, I sat down and wrote a letter of resignation, it was obvious, they never expected me to resign, over the next couple of weeks, several of the Brands top brass paid me a visit, in the hope that I would change my mind, to be fair they all praised me highly, explaining how well I had done, and all the plans I had put forward were now earmarked to be carried out in the foreseeable future, it would be a great shame to not be able to see them come to fruition, I must say I felt good about what was being said, but once I have made my mind up that is it.

My wife Anne was devastated, I knew she didn't want me to resign, and deep down I sometimes wonder if I should have done, but Anne being the fantastic wife she is, went along with my decision, this put our lives in turmoil, what do I do? Where do we go?

I now had to tell the staff that I was leaving, they were devastated, word soon got round that I was leaving, I was amazed at the amount of people that let their feelings be felt by contacting Brands, in the end I believe a standard letter from Brands was put together, to inform them, that Snetterton Circuit, will continue to flourish with or without Rick Shortle.

Without Anne and myself knowing, the staff had organised a farewell party in the circuit Pub, as far as I was aware it was to be a low key affair with a few of the staff, just to say goodbye and have a drink or two, when Anne and I arrived, the place was full of staff, drivers, marshals, photographers, it was a most moving experience, I must admit that I did have a tear or two in my eye, I didn't realise until that moment how much everyone thought of us, and that memory will stay with us forever, Georgina did a poem, which I framed and it still hangs on our wall at home to this very day.

Leaving was awful, I hired a van to take what possessions we had, which wasn't much, as the rest was still in storage, I remember the staff all outside the office ready to say their goodbyes, I think most of them had a tear in their eye, even Mick the maintenance Man, something I would never had believed, unless I actually saw it, we hugged the girls, poor Maria was crying her eyes out, Anne and I hopped into the van and drove away, it was the most horrible feeling, just as if we had lost a friend forever, Snetterton Circuit.

Chapter 23.
1992 Moving on.

We sold our bungalow when I took the Managers job, so we had to find rented accommodation, but where? Luckily for me I was still well know in the industry, their fore finding work didn't pose to much difficulty, it was decided if we live a bit more in the middle of England, commuting would be much easier, as the job would take me to every Race Circuit in the Country. We ended up in Hitchin Herts., but not for long, the house we rented was not bad, but the neighbours were diabolical, there was a postage stamp of a garden which back right next to a very busy roundabout, the fumes, and drone of the vehicles was too much, so within a couple of months we were gone.

Don't ask me how, but we ended up in Horsham West Sussex, up to now Anne had been working for Tesco, and managed to get a placement each time we moved, but unfortunately not this time, she went through a bad patch for a while, not being able to find work, she hated being at home doing nothing, but eventually found a job in the Bakers Oven, before getting a job in Waitrose, and is still working for them to this day.

I was busy going around the country working for all the car manufacturers, money was good, downside, always away, it was now 1994, the year I decided to hang up my helmet. A large proportion of my work was for Drive and Survive, who at the time were heavily involved with Ford, D&S were based at Boreham Essex, it was an old airfield which was ideal, most of their Corporate days up to now, involved driving or being driven around the airfield, which was turned into a circuit, and proved to be a super fast track the guests loved, at times it wasn't that enjoyable for us instructors, there is nothing worse than being driven on one of these Corporate days, by some blithering idiot, that hasn't got a clue, but think they have, I can tell you being a passenger, when your guest loses control at speed, is not funny.

At least we always got our own back, when at the end of the day, we would load them up in the cars and take them round, just to show them how it should be done, for them it was an eye opener, for us it was a relief to be in control.

On one occasion whilst working for D&S I popped into their workshops for a nose, I was quite intrigued why they had half a dozen almost new Go Karts stacked away in the corner, so me being me asked the MD, a Mr Andy Neal that very question, to which he explained, it was something they tried to do, but never had the expertise to make it happen properly, so they have ended up redundant, piled up in the back of the workshop, I asked Andy what did they actually try and do with them, they never had a proper kart track, he said the karts were part of their

Corporate Days, they would race each other on a make shift oval, it was ok until a couple or sometime even more got damaged, or broke down, it then became difficult and sometimes impossible to make them last the whole event, so they decided not to continue.

I could see an opportunity here, I gave it some thought for a couple of days, then decided to put a proposal to Andy Neal, at the time they were getting extremely busy with their Corporate Events, I sold him the idea of reinstating the karts back into his Events, but not with him having the headache of running them, no I would do that, I would charge D&S so much an event, but at a reduced price, and would always give him precedence over any other customer, if he was prepared to sell me the karts at a real knocked down price, Andy didn't hesitate, we did a deal there and then.

Fortunately for me D&S were about to relocate, to (TRL). Transport Research Laboratories at Crowthorne. Andy would be renting quite a number of offices and out buildings, located alongside the areas they would be using for their Events, he allowed me to use one of the garages free of charge, until I got on my feet, which was brilliant...

It wasn't long before business started to trickle in, D&S were giving me at least a couple of Events a week, which was better than nothing, I got myself a little brochure printed, started advertising in the Yellow Pages, and hey presto, work started to flood in, at this moment in time we were still operating with a makeshift oval, on an area which could quite easily become a fairly decent Kart Track, so off I go again, put my idea of constructing a proper go karting track, to Andy, which he thought was great, but this time it wasn't up to Andy, we had to go to TRL themselves, so did just that, the guy we dealt with was a Peter Young MBE, the Track Manager, I never expected to hear a yes. But a yes it was, there would now be the little matter of paying rent, and the deal we got was unbelievable, instead of paying so much a month, we only paid when we used it, now that is what I call the real deal.

As well as the track at TRL, I was doing mobile events, this was a very lucrative part of our business, I purchased a seven ton lorry, which was filled with car tyres they were shrink wrapped in red white and blue, when we arrived at our destination we would unload them and form an oval, this looked very colourful, with the flags and bunting, it was a good addition to any Corporate Event, I landed a Contract with a Company by the name of Fusion, they were based at Millbrook, which was very similar to TRL. Fusion did nothing but corporate events, they even had Helicopters, the guests would get a chance to take the controls, and in their heyday, they could do as many as four events a week, a great money spinner.

Things were going so well, I decided it was time to get a Manager for the Crowthorn Track, I knew the chap I wanted, a Noel Wilson, it was someone I used, to run the events at Crowthorn, he was a good all rounder, he could run the events, repair the karts, and maintain the track, and he was as honest as they come, I asked him if he fancied the job, the only problem was, he lived in Milton Keynes, which is nearly a hundred miles away, so part of the package would be to find him accommodation, Noel very quickly became a vital part of the organisation, he had a bloody good head on his shoulders, and loads of good ideas.

We got to work and constructed the track in a couple of weeks, and it turned out to be a cracker, once word got around, the business took off, within a few months, we were running events every day, a couple of our most lucrative events were the Mobility Road Show, which was extremely hard work but very rewarding, Noel adapted the karts, so they could be driven by drivers with all sorts of disabilities, he even bolted a type of sidecar to one of the karts, which would allow the most severely disabled to have a go, whilst Noel sat in the sidecar assisting.

Assisting a disabled Person into a kart at the Mobility Roadshow. Crowthorne.

Another event was the Volkswagen Owners Club, which we did on an arrive and drive basis; so much a lap, this was great fun, Anne and our Daughter Julia would take the money, Julia in particular was very good at getting them to part with their dosh, they would say 50p a lap or 10 laps for a fiver, it was always 10 laps they purchased, as most thought they were getting a good deal, they sometimes asked the girls which is the best kart, Anne or Julia would say the yellow one, they were all yellow he he! We met some really strange people on this event, one in particular, he was a strange looking charactor, looked like a tramp, had a long unruly beard, and a couple of bulging carrier bags, probably containing all his worldly goods, he produced a black marker pen, and asked me to write stop and go on the relative tops of his white trainers, so he knew which pedal to push, obviously this didn't work at all, he spent most of the time looking at his feet, and the rest of the time crashing, he was a bloody liability, so I had to ask him to leave.

Yes business was going extremely well, Noel was now in charge at the Crowthorne Track, I had set up office at home, which was a charming old dwelling by the name of Goat Cottage, in Nutborne Common, Pullborough, West Sussex, our tiny garden looked out over the rolling fields, which was only separated by the thinnest of a wire fence, it was just like an extension to our garden, and without doubt the most beautiful view you could ever wish for. I enjoyed working in my office, every day was a challenge, I was never happy unless I reached my daily target.

We were fortunate to run events for quite a few Celebrities, such as Tiff Needle, Top Gear, Sharon Davies the Swimmer, Alistair Stuart, in the TV serious, Police Camera Action, to name but a few.

Alistair Stewart. Police Camera Action

Tiff Needle Top Gear

But the icing on the cake was none other than, Tom Cruise, I was driving home one afternoon from Millbrook having finished an event for fusion, when my mobile rang, the caller said he was a Director for one of the big film companies, he explained they were filming part of that picture next to our kart track at Crowthorne, he went onto say that one of his actors has requested a run round in the karts, and would it be possible for him to do it that evening, I just said I'm sure we could sort something out, could he let me have the name of the actor, so I can inform security at the main gate, that he would be coming in, as I have to give the names of everyone that enters the site, he said, it will be Tom Cruise and his Son Conner, I remarked pull the other one, but he was quite serious, sure enough it was Tom Cruise, he was such a nice bloke, nothing at all aloof about him, he listened to everything we said, and a very good driver, in fact he broke the lap record, and held it for 2 years, he enjoyed himself so much, he hired the track for three evening on the trot, I think Tom was so unassuming, because we treated him exactly like we would every other guest, when in that sort of environment, it is hard to believe he was one of the World's leading film stars, Tom even allowed us to take a few pictures of him, we did try to get him to wear one of our karting tee-shirts, but unfortunately, didn't quite manage to get him to do that. It transpired. The Director was Stanley Kubrick, and the Film was Eyes Wide Shut. There's something to tell the Grandchildren. Needless to say I have a photo of Tom, standing next to me, alongside our track, which is framed, and on the wall at home.

Tom Cruise and Myself, at the Crowthorn Kart Track.

Sadly after three years I was informed by TRL that the area of land I was allocated, was to be developed into small industrial units, because I only paid for the time used, I never had a lease, it was theirfore, easy for them to give me notice, this was a devastating blow, our little empire was running like clockwork, to be fair I always had a feeling it may end like this, we were given six months notice which in the circumstances was more than could be expected, this meant I had to look for an alternative, fortunately I was already in consultation with the Tower Hamlets Environment Trust, they were looking to open a kart track in the East End of London, it was proposed to build the track on a waste piece of ground, right next to Burdett Road in Mile End, alongside several railway arches, which would be converted into a workshop, offices and briefing area, it was a kart track with a difference, the karts had to be Electric, which was a very new concept, very few karting centres ran electric karts, there were so many pit falls to get over, but I felt it could work, the deal was, Tower Hamlets would construct the track, complete with refurbished arches, I would then lease it, providing I used mainly local staff, I agreed, so work began ,but when you are involved with such a large establishment, things take ages to come together, in fact it took nearly three years from concept to fruition.

I have to admit when it was finished, it was fantastic, I was looking forward to getting the thing operating, and in July 2000 we opened, and that's when the trouble began, our very first event was ruined by a gang of youths, that jumped over the fence, which separated us from Burdett Road, we had to stop the event and call the police, sadly this was something that happened on a regular occurrence, we would get threatened by individuals coming in, and warning us, if we didn't do what we were told to do, they would make our lives hell, it was absolutely awful, even some of the staff would smoke joints openly, I persevered for a couple of years, I was always having to drive to the track in the middle of the night, the police would call to say the alarm went off due to a break in, we had karts stolen, windows smashed, even a fire was started, and the final straw that broke the Camel's back, was when I was held up with a gun, I ended up with a minder, this all proved too much, and ended up with a nervous breakdown, I had enough, so I put it up for sale, I was glad to get rid of it. How sad! it should have been a roaring success, it was too much of a culture shock for me, I still can't understand why certain people are like that, I had found my weakness, in being unable to control those sort of people, when I walked away I never looked back, and to this very day I am not at all interested, in how this track has progressed, it has probably done very well, particularly if it is run by local people, that understand and can cope.

I was in quite a mess for a few months, the doctor put me on happy pills, which calmed me down, Anne said I was away with the fairies, I did nothing apart from sitting around being useless to everyone around me, slowly I recovered, and felt I should try to find a job, any job that may help with my recovery, as long it didn't involved any sort of responsibility, I found just the job down the road washing cars, the money was crap, but it was certainly instrumental in putting me on the road to recovery.

It wasn't long before I got a telephone call from someone that knew me, he asked if I would be interested in going into business with him, to run an indoor karting centre in Colchester, I gave it some thought, and decided to give it a go. After a couple of years I felt the passion for this type of business was no longer for me, so I parted company with him, and decided this was to be the last time I would ever run, own, or be involved in a karting business ever again.

Chapter 24.
2004 – 2010 Full Circle.

I enjoyed my time at Colchester, but felt the time was right to leave, to be honest I recon I may have left sooner, but my Mum had become seriously ill, she lived in Clacton which is only 15mins away from Colchester, she was in hospital for her final weeks, so I was able to go and see her every day until she passed away, God bless her.

On my way home, which was Boxworth, Cambridge, I didn't have a clue what was in store, I was reminiscing of all that was, and strangely enough I wasn't sad, but looking forward to the next chapter, as I almost reached home I decided to stop and fill up with petrol, whilst paying, I grabbed a free job search magazine, jump back in the car and made the short drive home. It was a strange feeling as I pulled into the drive, knowing my life was about to change.

Anne was still at work, so I made myself a cup of tea, and started flicking through this job search magazine, I came to the building trade page, and noticed a local builder was looking for plumbers, electricians, and a plasterer, bearing in mind I hadn't worked as a plasterer for over twenty years, but as usual me being me, decided to give them a call, to apply for the position, I explained, that I hadn't done plastering for a very long time, but looking to get away from what I currently do, I was prepared to work at a reduced rate until they were happy, he said well! we are busy, why don't you meet me at the job, we need you for, and take it from there. I met Jim one of the Managers, the next afternoon, it was a Friday, he showed me the job, and agreed to give me a start, which was on the Monday, I had no tools, and so off I went and purchased what I needed.

I was quite excited about the whole affair, not bad, two days, and back at work, but this time as a plasterer, I had gone "full circle", back where I was years ago, I can tell you I was very nervous, could I do the job, its hard work? will I like it? I will certainly find out on Monday.

Monday morning, and off I go, on site were two chippies (Carpenters) they were very friendly and extremely helpful, My first task was a couple of ceilings, these are without doubt the hardest to do, and for a few days after, I could hardly move my neck, ceilings really do take it out of you, so until my neck got stronger I had to put up with the discomfort, I very soon became accepted within the company, they even supplied me with a van, which I filled up with diesel from their yard, so travelling expenses were covered.

I continued working for them, for a couple of years on the cards. In the meantime we decided to move to a little village called Woodford, in Northamptonshire, to be nearer our youngest daughter Julia, our new home was a little cottage at the foot of a hill, which overlooks the church, Julia lives about a minute away at the top of the hill, it was lovely to be near one of our Daughters again, sadly our other Daughter Tina, lives miles away, in Oxted, Surrey, but we do try to visit as often as possible.

Now that we lived in Woodford, I was finding it more and more tasking, travelling to the builders jobs, so I decided to put an advertisement in the local church magazine, to try and generate local business, I stayed with the builder for another year, and doing any plastering jobs that came along from the ad at weekends, that year proved to be very hard, but it paid dividends. By the end of the year I had enough plastering jobs coming in, to make it possible to leave the builder. I have been fortunate enough to find ample work; in a small village like this, it's all word of mouth, in the five years we have been here, I have worked in 65 houses in Woodford alone, I still do the odd driving job, but pick and choose what I wish to do.

Plastering an arch for a customer

Recieving an Award for Plastering.

We have been here for 5 years, and both Anne and I agree this is the best place we have ever lived, we couldn't wish for better neighbours, we get on so well, there's Jane and Dick one side and Jane and Dave the other, which does get a bit confusing sometimes, even more so, when we have the odd drink. We find, now we have slowed down a bit, we do get much more time to visit, in particular Anne's Sisters' Brenda and Hazel. Hazel and Husband Charlie, are always visiting, Charlie like me, loves a tipple, we have a right laugh when we get together, it's good to see Brenda and her other half Bernard, once you start seeing people again, you feel a little annoyed with yourselves, that you didn't try just a bit harder earlier.. Although! I'm so pleased that we always made as much free time as we could, to visit our parents, all sadly passed away, but never forgotten.

Anne's Dad Andrew and dear Bet at her ninetieth Birthday Party.

It's now 2010, although we certainly cannot afford to retire, Anne is only working three days a week, yes still at Waitrose, and I try, not to do much more, but in a village it's hard if not impossible, as I do not want to let anyone down

To me my life has been extremely interesting, and it still is; now we have the privilege of seeing our Grandchildren grow up, as a parent with all that was going on, me in particular, I missed so much of both Tina and Julia growing up, for which I apologise, Anne without doubt was the catalyst in making our two lovely Daughters what they are today, both are a credit two us, we couldn't have wished for anything better. We are delighted with their Husbands, both are very hands on, Nick can cook fantastic meals, Jason is very caring, and looks after Cameron as if he is his own, they are both proper Dads

Anne's recent Birthday Party with a sixties theme.

Julia on the left, Tina on the right, us two old codgers in the middle.

They have given us four fantastic Grandchildren. There's Tina and Nick.

Thomas, a little 8 year old that exhumes confidence in everything he does, he loves football rugby, and his biggest claim to fame so far, is playing the small boy in Billy

Elliot, the Musical, in London's Victoria Palace, and dear Bethan a cheeky, loving 7 year old, who loves dancing and swimming, in 2011 she will swim for the school.

Then we have Julia and Jason.

Cameron, nearly 10, his Dad is Fraser, a former partner of Julia, It's great that Cameron spends lots of time with his real Dad, they get on so well, Fraser is a keen footie fan just like his Son, Cameron is the Goalkeeper for the under tens, and shows a lot of promise, he was awarded Managers Player of the Year,2010, strangely enough I was the goalkeeper for the school at that age.

And then we have Matthew, just two, and without doubt, the best behaved two year old I have ever seen, he's as bright as a button, a cheeky, cutie, little rascal, even at that age, he knows how to get round his Grand dad bless him.

The Family.
Top of table Rick and Anne.
Lefthand side of table, starting with furthest away.
Cameron-Thomas-Tina Righthand side of table, starting with furthest away.
Julia-Jason holding Matthew -Nick Nearest-Bethan

So there we have it, my life so far, I would like to say, I now look forward to the next 60 years, but sadly I can't, but what I will say is, I certainly intend to live my life to the full, with my lovely wife Anne, whom I thank for being just Anne.

We both look forward to spending much more time with our Daughters, and Son-in-Laws, as well as seeing our Grand Kids grow up and amaze us on a daily basis.

Lightning Source UK Ltd.
Milton Keynes UK
UKHW012005180521
383946UK00001B/50